GENGHIS KHAN
AND THE MONGOL HORDE

GENGHIS KHAN

AND THE

MONGOL HORDE

BY HAROLD LAMB

Illustrated by ELTON FAX

Printed in the United States of America.

First Sonlight Curriculum, Ltd. Edition, 2000.

1 3 5 7 9 8 6 4 2
01 03 05 07 08 06 04 02 00

ISBN 1-887840-38-9

For a catalog of Sonlight Curriculum materials for the home school, write:

Sonlight Curriculum, Ltd.
8042 South Grant Way
Littleton, CO 80122-2705
USA

Or e-mail: catalog@sonlight.com

CONTENTS

Once a man almost conquered all the earth. He did make himself master of half our world, more than seven hundred years ago. They called him Genghis Khan.

No man's name, before or since his time, has been so terrible to living people. No one else has been quite like him. Sometimes he seemed to be more than human in his power. He seemed to be like the storm wind that swept out of his deserts, tearing up the cities in its path.

So people spoke of him then. This is the story of who he really was, and how he came to leave his home.

It was far beyond Europe, far to the east of the familiar world, out where the caravan tracks led to the bare Gobi Desert. . . .

GENGHIS KHAN
AND THE MONGOL HORDE

1

Under the North Wind

THEY RODE CROUCHED FORWARD IN THE SADDLE. The boy's father led the way as they searched for the lost horse. At times they glanced out at the haze along the skyline.

All around them the plain swelled and sank, yellow with dead grass. The haze came from dust in the air, stirred up by the wind that pressed against their backs. Both the nine-year-old boy and his father knew that the stray horse would have kept moving downwind. The icy wind from the northern snow cut through the backs of their sheepskin jackets.

The boy's name was Temujin, which meant Iron. He was so accustomed to cold that he did not think about it. His sable fur cap with its leather flap protected his head and neck; his wide leather trousers were tucked into felt boots.

The mane of his shaggy pony had been clipped so that the wirelike hair would not be blown up into his eyes. He had rubbed his face with grease to shield his frost sores from the wind.

Something gray and swift flashed past Temujin, and his narrowed eyes turned to it instantly. It was only a dry thornbush, torn loose by the wind. But the nine-year-old boy was experienced enough to know that his father had enemies in grazing lands not far away. His father was a fighting man, and head of a clan, among the horse nomads.

It was not a large clan, theirs of the Yakka Mongols—the Great Mongols. The chieftains seemed to have a greater wealth of pride than of furs and good steel weapons. Temujin himself spent most of his time in the saddle, watching the herds while the grown men were off raiding or hunting. With his younger brothers, Temujin hunted the smaller game of the home pastures—the lean winter-dwelling animals like the sables, marmots, or black foxes. They ate the flesh and saved the sinews and skins.

Even their games were like strife. The nomad
folk had horse races—ten miles out over the
prairies and back; they had wrestling matches
in which bones were broken. When they killed
plenty of game they ate all the meat they could,
to keep off hunger for the lean days to come.

Temujin could go three or four days without
food. He often felt the ache of hunger before
he found food again. Sometimes he took his
knife, opened a vein in the horse he rode, and
drank some of its blood. Then he closed the
vein and went on.

Now he noticed faint tracks in the dry, sandy
earth. His father saw them, too, and turned
aside to follow them. Temujin waited a moment

and then said, "This herd is not ours. It grazed here before the wind came up."

"I know that," his father replied. "Our horse joined it. The herd went to shelter when the wind came."

Temujin was not so sure of that. But he could not object when his father had decided a thing. He had to obey the leader of the clan. On the barren plains, accidents or death happened too easily to nomad riders who did not act together.

After a few minutes they sighted the herd, crowded together with tails to the wind, in a hollow behind standing rocks. Their missing gray horse with the white blaze was in the thick of the herd.

Beyond the herd, tents took shape in the haze. Beside them stood wide empty wagons. These round leather tents, shaped like domes, had been taken from the wagons and set up on the ground.

Carefully Temujin's father scanned the encampment and the tethered riding horses. Then he reined forward and dismounted. These were strange folk but no known enemies.

When darkness came, the two Mongol riders were seated by a glowing fire of thornbush

They had been placed at the right hand, the side of honor, of the master of the tents. Women brought in and set before them steaming caldrons of millet boiled with sheep bones.

"We have little to offer," said their host.

"At the end of winter," replied Temujin's father, "this is much."

Among the women Temujin noticed a small girl with bright, dark eyes. She moved about quickly without noise, smoothing out a red carpet that must have come from some caravan; she took a bone from the pot and carried it to the closed entrance flap, where she let it touch the wooden image hanging there. This was the household image of a spirit rider of the Sky.

Then the ten-year-old girl put the meat bone back in the pot, and her dark eyes gleamed with pleasure.

The owner of the tent noticed that the boy kept watching his young daughter. Eying the Mongol father and son, he told them she would make a good wife.

Suddenly Temujin asked if he could have her for a wife. He had a way of doing things swiftly like that—of becoming angry or fired with a new purpose.

His father looked at the girl and asked her name. It was Bortay, which meant that she had gray eyes. "She is young," he objected.

But Temujin was sure that he wanted her. "When she is older," he pointed out, "she will do well enough."

When her name was spoken, Bortay went to kneel quietly by the older women. It was easy to see that she had been well brought up.

"She is small," her father observed, "but still you might look at her."

Secretly he was pleased by the interest the visiting Mongols took in her. The chieftain of the Yakka Mongols had several thousand family tents following him over the grasslands. So Bortay's father looked approvingly at the boy Temujin. "Your son has a clear face and bright eyes," he said.

The older men sat up until late that night, to strike the bargain about the marriage. It was decided that after a few years Temujin's father would pay the bride-price of so many head of horses, oxen and sheep. Although it was settled between them, it did not happen as they had expected.

The next day the windstorm ceased and Temujin's father led away their gray horse. The Mongol chieftain had to visit other settlements. He left Temujin with Bortay's father, to become better acquainted.

At such a time, when snow swept the steppes and the wild fowl no longer came out of the sky to the frozen lakes, wandering minstrels were apt to ride in. They were old men, sometimes blind, who sang with droning voices the tales of a tribe's ancestors.

Such legends Temujin stored away in his memory. Like most of the nomads, he could neither read nor write. He had to make a map in his mind of the trails that led to higher ground and better grass in the heat of the summer, or to watering places in the sandy stretches of the Gobi.

Now a minstrel with a fiddle came by. He sang the tale of an ancestral chieftain who had pulled the emperor of Cathay by the beard and had been poisoned as a result.

Afterward it seemed strange to Temujin that the minstrel had chosen that tale to tell. Temujin himself had never so much as seen the trading caravans of laden camels that passed along the Pe Lu, the Great North Road, going east to the gates in the Wall.

That Wall had been built by the Chinese long before, to keep the horse nomads from raiding their empire. They called the remote tent-dwellers Tartars and Greasy Ones.

In Cathay, Temujin's father had said, the people possessed so much wealth that they lived in houses of brick and stone. He said the tribes of the Gobi were safe from the power of Cathay only because they dwelt far away in lands too barren to be desired by the emperors behind the Wall.

Temujin thought of his words. "We are not a hundredth part of Cathay. The only reason we have withstood her is that we are all nomads carrying our supplies about with us. We are experienced in our kind of warfare. When we can, we plunder what we need; when we cannot, we hide away. If we began to build towns and change our old habits we would fall into misfortune."

Because of the minstrel's song, the boy had his father's words in his mind. Then a rider came in with news that the Mongol chieftain had

When Temujin arrived, he found his father dead.

fallen sick in the tents of an enemy. Perhaps he had been poisoned.

Although the boy rode to the place as fast as a horse could carry him, he found his father dead. No one would say how he died. There was nothing to do but bring his body back on a cart.

In his own encampment most of the warriors were talking together and deciding to leave.

"The deep water that strengthened us is gone," they said. "The strong stone that protected us is broken. What have we to do with a woman and her children?"

Their loaded wagons began to trundle away from the camp. They were afraid to trust themselves and their families to a woman and an inexperienced boy like Temujin.

The boy's anxious mother did what she could to keep the clan from breaking up. She took the pole with the nine white yak tails—the standard of the Mongol Khan—and went out to the deserters, pleading with them to stay. Only a few did so.

As the eldest son, Temujin had to decide what his family should do. For a while he sat grieving by the embers within the hearthstones.

Behind the hearth stretched the white horse-hide that had been the seat of the Khan.

Then Temujin told his mother that he would take the Khan's place. The family would stay with its herds and possessions in its home pastures by the two rivers.

That meant they would all have to defend themselves against the dead chieftain's enemies, who would surely come to take vengeance on the children.

2

Night Attack

THE FIRST HOSTILE RAIDERS CAME SILENTLY AT the end of a night. They were all mounted and armed. When their scouts reached the outmost herds of the Yakka Mongol encampment, they waited for all the riders to come up before rushing the camp.

They were the Taidjuts, a strong neighboring clan. Above everything they wanted to gain for themselves the wide grazing lands of Temujin's father—grasslands watered by the small rivers and melting snow. In the low hills covered with birch and fir, plenty of game could be found.

So, while some of the Taidjut riders rounded up the outer herds, most of them headed straight for Temujin's tent. It was marked by the standard pole with the nine white tails. Since Temujin claimed these prairies as his own, the Taidjuts wanted to kill or capture him.

As they rode in they shot flights of arrows through the Mongol tents. In warfare like this, the horse nomads showed little mercy to the weak.

Temujin had been asleep in his *yurt*—the round tent of haircloth stretched over a framework of tied poles and whitened with lime on the outside. Its only opening, except for the hole in the top to let smoke out, was an entrance on the sunny side. Temujin ran out and hurried his brothers and sisters to the place where horses were being saddled for them.

He was easily distinguished from the other children by his long red hair and high, stooping shoulders. It is said that he had gray-green eyes and was quick to see in the dark, like a cat. He was rather thin but could throw the strongest boy wrestlers. And he moved quickly, with the cunning of an animal.

One of his brothers, a strong archer called the Bowman, tried to stand and fight with his bow. But Temujin made all the children flee at a gallop from the *yurts*. Only his mother could not escape. The few Mongol warriors who had stayed with Temujin were scattering, their herds lost.

The Taidjuts made no great haste to follow the children. Those nomads were accustomed to tracking down a horse for days if necessary. So long as Temujin did not get a fresh mount, they could close in on him after daybreak.

The boys headed for the shelter of a ravine in the hills. They could ride as well as grown men, for they had learned as babies to stay on the back of a sheep by holding to the wool. They knew how to feed themselves by catching fish in the streams and hunting small game like hares and marmots. When they stopped to rest their horses, Temujin made them cut down a tree leaning over the narrow trail, to hinder the pursuers. Yet the Taidjuts were close behind them.

At twilight the children separated. The younger ones and the girls hid in a cave. The Bowman went one way, and Temujin another —toward the highest hill. This was dark with dense forest, and people called it the Mountain of Power.

Here Temujin kept away from the pursuers for days.

Then hunger made him try to slip through the watching Taidjuts, leading his horse. He was seen and caught. To keep him from escaping the Taidjuts fastened a *kang* to his shoulders. This was a heavy wooden yoke which fitted around his neck and to which his wrists were bound at either end.

Yet Temujin did escape. The Taidjuts were driving back the captured herds to their village. One evening they held a feast and left the yoked boy alone with a single guard. When it was dark he managed to strike the armed warrior on the head with the end of the *kang*. Running from the campfires, he found himself in a grove of trees lighted by a rising moon.

Temujin plunged through the brush, then made his way toward a river they had crossed the day before. The wooden yoke hindered him and he heard warriors coming after him. Running hard, he reached the water and let himself sink into the rushes that lined the bank of the river. Only his head projected above the water.

When the Taidjut riders searched the bank for him, he noticed that one warrior saw him. The man hesitated and then went on without betraying him.

Bound as he was to the *kang*, Temujin realized that his situation was critical. When the riders turned back to wait for daylight before tracking him down, Temujin took a desperate chance. From his hiding place he followed them back to the camp and crept to the *yurt* of the warrior who had seen him in the rushes but had spared him.

As it happened this man was not a Taidjut but

The boy still had the wooden yoke on his shoulders.

a stranger who had joined the clan on the march. At sight of the dripping boy crawling to the embers of his fire, the man was more frightened than was Temujin. He felt pity for the hunted captive and at the same time he wanted to get rid of him.

The stranger split the *kang* and burned the wooden parts. Then he hid Temujin in a nearby cart loaded with loose wool.

When the angered Taidjuts searched the encampment the next day, they thrust their lances into the wool, and a blade wounded Temujin in the leg. He made no sound.

"The smoke of my house would have vanished forever if they had found you," the strange warrior remarked grimly to Temujin when he helped him out of the cart after dark. "Go away now to your mother and brothers."

With that he gave the boy some food and sour milk, and a bow with two arrows. Thus fed and armed, Temujin led out a horse and got away over the prairies.

Still hiding by day, he searched for and found his mother and the other children. They had only a few men left to serve them and only nine horses among them all.

He might have fled with the family from their ancestral grazing grounds beneath the Mountain of Power. They might have claimed shelter with several far-off powerful chieftains, the friends of Temujin's father. But he would not do that. He chose, instead, to hide out in the home prairies of his two river valleys.

"To go forth as a beggar with empty hands," Temujin argued, "is to arouse scorn, not friendship."

So he stayed. For several years the family lived on fish and small game, not mutton. Yet Temujin went the rounds of the *yurts* of warriors who had served his father, the Khan of the Yakka Mongols. At each settlement he gravely claimed the Khan's tithe, or tax, of four beasts —a camel, ox, horse and sheep. It did not seem to the warriors that they should pay this tithe to a fugitive boy who could not defend them.

Still Temujin insisted that he was their Khan.

Meanwhile, eight of his horses were stolen.

3

Tracking the Horses

PROWLING TAIDJUTS HAD TAKEN THE HORSES. OF course Temujin could not follow on foot. He waited until one of his brothers rode in on a tired sorrel mare with some marmots he had hunted and killed.

When he heard about the stolen horses, this brother said he would follow them on the mare.

"You could not find them," Temujin objected.

"I can follow and find them," promised his strong brother, the Bowman.

"You could not bring them back," Temujin objected again. "I will go after them."

So he started out on the track of the horses, riding the tired sorrel mare and armed with his brother's bow. When the red-haired Temujin became angry like this, his brothers knew it was useless to argue with him.

And Temujin knew he had to get the stolen herd back. These horse nomads had no money, or farms, or houses. They were forced to struggle to keep alive on the great plains. Even their food—meat and milk—came from their animals. From wool they made the covering of their beehive-shaped *yurts,* which sheltered them during blizzards; from split sinews they made ropes and lariats. They strengthened their bows with horn.

Without horses to ride, they could not manage the herds of other animals, or travel fast to escape snow or drought in the desert.

Although he was alone, the boy kept on after the raiders for days, following the trail in the grass. But because his mare was tired, he could not catch up with the Taidjuts, who changed their saddles to fresh horses whenever they liked.

Temujin had taken some dried meat, putting it between his saddle and the mare's back to soften and warm it. After this was eaten he had no more food.

One day at sunrise the young Mongol came

up to a youth of his own age who was milking a mare beside the trail. In spite of his hunger, he did not ask for milk. "Have you seen eight horses and some men driving them?" he asked, reining in.

"Yes, before dawn eight driven horses went past me. I will show you the trail they took."

After another glance at the solitary Mongol, the strange youth tied up his leather milk sack and hid it in some tall grass. "You look tired and anxious," said he. "My name is Borchu, and I will ride with you after the horses."

"It will be easy enough to ride after them," Temujin told the friendly Borchu. "But to get them back will be like pulling thorns from flesh."

That did not change Borchu's mind. The tired sorrel was turned out to graze, and the strange youth roped and saddled a white horse from the herd he was tending. Riding this fresh white horse, Temujin pushed on quickly after the Taidjuts, his new companion beside him. They found the camp of the raiders and soon discovered the stolen horses grazing near by.

These the two youths drove off, and were promptly pursued by the warriors. One man, mounted on a white stallion and gripping a lariat, began to overtake them.

Borchu offered to take Temujin's bow and hang back to meet the pursuers, but Temujin would not let him. "These men might wound you," he said. "I will use the bow."

Daylight was beginning to fail by then. The rider of the white stallion pressed closer, swinging his lariat rope. Dropping back, Temujin turned suddenly in the saddle and loosed an arrow at him. The Taidjut fell to the ground, and the others drew rein when they came up to him.

The two youths hurried on through the night to the camp of Borchu's father. On the way Borchu picked up the sack of milk he had hidden. He showed the eight horses to his father and explained why he had gone after them. "When I saw him weary and anxious, I went with him."

The father, who was master of a large herd himself, listened attentively to the boys' story. They had done a hard thing in bringing horses away safely from an armed camp. "You are both young," he told them. "Well, be friends—and faithful to each other."

With that he gave Temujin food and the sack

Temujin turned suddenly and loosed an arrow at him.

of mare's milk to take with him. But Temujin told Borchu that without him the horses could not have been found. And he offered Borchu four of the eight to keep for himself.

To this Borchu would not agree. "If I should take what is yours to pay myself, how could you call me a friend?"

A few days later he rode over to the young Mongol's camp with a gift of black fox fur for the family, and offered to follow Temujin faithfully.

Since these riders of the plains never made use of writing, they were careful to keep a spoken promise. The red-haired Temujin was no exception. At times he would fall into fits of anger, but he shared generously all he had with those who, like Borchu, came in to help him. He showed them how few belongings he had— how few stacks of furs, and leather chests of clothing and weapons. "A merchant trusts in his goods that he can sell for a profit," he said. "My people trust only in their cunning and strength."

After a few years it began to be said, from the Mountain of Power to the sands of the Gobi Desert, that Temujin and his comrades were growing in strength. They could escape from their enemies by putting their *yurts* on great wide-wheeled carts that yoked oxen drew slowly over the grasslands.

But Temujin could not yet protect any other people. Although he insisted stubbornly that he was Khan of the Yakka Mongols, he could not keep invaders out of their ancestral pastures. Under those conditions his people might forget about his father and choose an older man to defend them in war. Yet his young comrades like Borchu swore that they would serve no one but him.

By his watchfulness and cunning, rather than by his strength, Temujin kept them all alive. For he had only a small clan to follow him among the mighty hordes of the other nomads.

When he was seventeen, Temujin made his first attempt to claim his father's friends for allies. At least he could go to them not as a beggar but as a leader with horsemen of his own following him.

The first thing he did was to make a journey to claim for his wife the girl who had been promised him in his father's time. He had not seen Bortay since she was a child.

His sudden appearance surprised everyone in her camp. Temujin had a way of moving unexpectedly across the steppes.

"When I heard how many enemies had gone against you," said Bortay's father as he greeted the young Khan, "we did not expect to see you again alive."

Not only was Temujin alive but more than a hundred young warriors cantered up behind him—riders in fur-edged leather jackets with crude breastplates of hard lacquered leather. They wore lances behind their shoulders, and kits were slung on the cruppers of their high saddles. All of them were dusty and joyful and hungry.

Bortay's father feasted them in token of his welcome. Sheep and horses were killed for meat. The warriors filled themselves with food, sitting by the older men at the *yurt* fires. They drank sour milk and rice wine, and danced in their soft boots when the musicians played one-string fiddles.

It was a festival for small, slender Bortay as well. She had waited years for Temujin's coming, and she was now eighteen years old.

The older women of the encampment dressed

the girl in white wool, putting heavy silver coins in her dark hair and a wedding cap of birch bark covered with silk upon her head.

After the wedding feast they tied blue streamers of silk around Bortay. They set her on a horse to ride away while her brothers and sisters went through the play of struggling with Temujin to keep him from following her. They called this carrying off the bride.

Temujin managed to elude her people and to ride off after Bortay. Her servants brought along a fine sable cloak as a gift for his mother.

When they rode away joyfully that day, neither Temujin nor Bortay had ever ventured out of their prairie land. They knew the trails only from the Mountain of Power to the dry sands of the Gobi. Of the outer world they had heard only from masters of passing caravans and minstrels.

Yet three of their sons were destined to rule most of that outer world.

4

The Battle of the Carts

LIKE THE FRONTIER WOMEN OF EARLY AMERICA,
Bortay, young as she was, had to take charge
of Temujin's tents. No sooner had she tied up
her long hair in braids around her head than
she had to see to it, as the wife of the Khan, that
all the people who served him were fed, cared
for and clothed. "Every mouth must be fed,"
his mother told her.

These women wove cloth out of wool and hair;
they made the hearth fires out of dried animal
dung; they packed away all the scraps of food.
When the warriors were off hunting or raiding,
the women and older children had to ride herd
on the precious animals.

Being horse nomads, the Yakka Mongols and
Bortay's people were the proudest of the steppe

dwellers—the grassland folk. Keepers of cattle were looked up to most after the horse owners. Then came the sheep herders, the forest hunters and trappers of the snow tundras in the north. Lowest of all were those who dug in the earth to grow food crops. But few farmers had ever come into the wind-swept steppes.

Bortay and the other women sowed a little grain along the river banks. They did not know if they could stay long enough at that place to harvest the grain. For when drought came and the grass began to die, Temujin and the old, experienced men—the *sechens*—would watch the sky for days. Then they would decide where they had all better go to find the fresh grass their herds needed in order to live.

So any day the women might be told to pack all belongings and prepare to take up the trail again. All the Mongol clothing and utensils fitted into small leather chests or into what we would call blanket rolls. Everything had to be loaded on animal-back or into the wheeled wagons that were pulled by twenty oxen.

Once the Mongols were on the trail, Temujin had to manage to graze the herds and to bring in food for thousands of human beings. He could not rest, because he was responsible for the life of everyone.

The worst danger on the prairies came from the winter blizzards when the north wind swept across frozen Lake Baikul.

Men who were caught out on the range in such a blizzard would try to lie down in their fur coverings beside a snow drift that broke the force of the wind. Once when Temujin lay like that through a night, he found that two of his heroes had stood over him holding a leather blanket to ward off the wind.

"I will remember," he told them, "how the two of you gave me life by keeping off the wind."

When they got back safely to the encampment after the storm, Temujin lay down by the warmth of his hearth and slept as though dead. The sound of Bortay weeping roused him. She was kneeling by him and crying. "If evil befell you," she whispered, "what would become of me and all the small children?"

Yet it was Bortay who was lost to Temujin soon after their marriage.

The Merkits, a savage people up in the northern tundras, had an old grievance against Temujin's family. In their homeland, called "the frozen white world," the Merkits hunted fur-bearing animals; in winter they used reindeer to draw sledges over the snow trails.

During one winter they migrated south to the prairies. There they searched out the Mongol encampment. At night they raided it, throwing blazing torches into the tents.

Temujin was able to get to a horse and escape, clearing his way with arrows. But Bortay was carried off by the Merkit raiders and given to one of their warriors. By this act they thought they had wiped out their old grudge against Temujin's kin.

Temujin knew his clan was not strong enough to ride against the Merkits. So in his anxiety he did what he had not been willing to do before. He appealed for help to a more powerful chieftain.

This chieftain was Toghrul Khan, and to reach him meant several days' journey to the west. Toghrul, old and peaceful, was Khan of a people quite different from the horse nomads. Dwelling closer to the caravan tracks, his people, the Keraits, traded more with the outer world. Many of them had become Christians.

When Temujin came to Toghrul Khan, he

brought as a gift the sable cloak that had been Bortay's present to her mother-in-law. Since the old Toghrul had been the friend of Temujin's father, the young man called the Kerait chieftain his foster father.

And Toghrul did not refuse his aid in taking vengeance on the Merkits. As he was too old to ride on an expedition himself, he let Temujin command the Kerait war bands as well as his own.

As soon as the snow left the prairies, the young Khan led his new army north. Using all his cunning, he approached the Merkit village, which was in a forest. There, he had learned, Bortay was held captive.

Cautiously he kept his horsemen in the forest out of sight of watchers until nightfall. Then he rode in swiftly. A rising moon gave light when the Mongol riders galloped through the disordered huts.

Those who watched Temujin that night said that he kept calling Bortay's name. When she ran out to catch his rein, they said he recognized her in the moonlight and dismounted at once, telling them, "I have found what I sought here."

So he brought Bortay safely home. Yet neither of them could forget her captivity among the Merkits. Her first child was a son. Temujin chose a strange name for the boy.

"He is welcome," the Khan said. "We will call him the Guest."

So the child's name became Juchi, the Guest.

Temujin had taken a dangerous step when he made himself the ally of the old and powerful Khan of the Keraits. Until then he had kept his people pretty much apart from others. Now he had mingled with the stronger peoples who strove for mastery over all the prairie land.

Of course he had friends now, toward the western caravan tracks. But in the east toward the mountain wall his old enemies, the Taidjuts, began to envy his new importance and at the same time to fear him. The Taidjuts also had allies, the dreaded Tartars of the Buyar Lake.

It seemed to the chieftains of the Taidjuts and Tartars that they had better get Temujin alone and do away with him. Together the Taidjut-Tartars were three times as strong as his Mongols.

They laid their plans to attack him un-

That night Temujin kept calling Bortay's name.

expectedly when he was on the march far away from his Kerait allies. In this way they could make themselves masters of the best river lands and of all Temujin's possessions as well.

They gathered together a great army for the attack.

At that time there were few soldiers who could face such an army of hard-riding horsemen as Temujin's. All these men of the steppes had been trained for war.

Although their weapons were light—slender lances, lariats and saddle axes and short, curved hacking swords—they were easily carried. These warriors had no heavy iron armor as did the knights and soldiers of the outer world. Hardened leather protected their bodies, as well as small round shields that fitted over their bow arms. Small helmets with leather drops protected their heads and necks.

Most important, they could ride vast distances without halting, and they could find food on the way instead of carrying it in clumsy packs.

Long before, a Roman soldier had noticed how terrifying the nomads of the steppes of Asia were on horseback. *"They even sleep leaning on the necks of their mounts,"* he wrote. *"Never do they cultivate a field or touch a plow. They wander always—small men afoot, but in the saddle seeming gigantic."*

One reason why they inspired such terror was their skill in using the short saddle bow. These bows, spliced with horn, were bent to great tension. Arrows flew from them almost with the speed of today's bullets.

When the riders were alert to danger, the bows were carried ready-strung in a case on one hip. The arrows hung stacked for use on the other hip. By a quick movement of both hands the rider could fit and shoot an arrow.

Through long experience these horsemen had learned the value of discipline. Each man had his place in a squad of ten, and the squad in a company of a hundred—in a regiment of a thousand. They learned to keep silence, guided by movements of lance pennants in daylight and colored lanterns at night. So they were rarely ever seen or heard until they burst upon an enemy like a whirlwind.

They had learned also to obey the orders of their khans. For example, although Borchu could walk at will into Temujin's tent or sit with him to share his food, he had to carry out any order the young Khan gave him. Temujin never forgave anyone who disobeyed him.

Such lifelong training helped Temujin preserve his people when the Taidjuts and Tartars descended on him in the battle of the carts.

On the day the enemy attacked, Temujin was leading his people on a migration down a long valley. He had perhaps thirteen thousand men following him, but they had their families in the *kibitkas*—the tent-wagons—and their herds grazing by the trail.

Scouts galloped in with the warning that thirty thousand enemy horsemen were coming over the skyline, heading for the valley.

Temujin had only a few moments to decide what to do. If he fled with his armed men, they would lose their families, cattle and possessions. If he charged out into the prairie, his small army would be surrounded and cut to pieces by the more numerous Taidjut-Tartars.

It looked as if his clan would be destroyed, in one way or the other. Swiftly Temujin prepared to do something different. No ordinary army could have done in such a short space of time what he made his people do. But the experienced horse nomads were accustomed to getting into their saddles and maneuvering like a flash.

They formed into a line of regiments facing the enemy, with a dense wood on one side. On the other side, the *kibitkas* were moved into a square, and women and children equipped with bows piled into them. At the same time, the cattle herds were driven into the square for protection.

So when the Taidjuts and Tartars swept down

into the valley, they found the Mongol regiments massed, ready and waiting between the forest and the square of carts. For a while the enemy charged, using their bows. But in that narrow space the Mongols could use just as many bows as could their foe.

Meanwhile, the relentless Temujin had been doing something else. Behind each regiment of a thousand warriors he put another one. Then, suddenly, he led out all his regiments to attack.

The most heavily armed riders, whose horses too wore leather armor, went in front. Of course Temujin had only six of the *double* regiments of cavalry against thirty of the enemy's. Yet the weight of the charge of the Mongols was so great that the lighter Taidjut-Tartars could not stand against it.

The charging Mongols separated and whirled as they rushed on after the standard with the nine white tails. They loosed arrows on either side as they drove into the enemy, who could not endure the terrible fighting and fled away to safety.

Up the valley the battle sped. When daylight ended, five or six thousand of the enemy had fallen. Seventy of their chieftains were led before Temujin, to kneel with swords and quivers hanging from their necks.

The young Khan had won a great victory over foemen more than twice as strong as he was. Word went over the steppes that Temujin was aided by the power of Heaven.

5

The Gathering of the Torrents

MORE THAN ANYTHING ELSE, THE MONGOLS feared this power of the everlasting Sky, as they called it. Out of the Sky came whirlwinds, thunder, lightning and blizzards. And out of the Sky came the life-giving warmth of spring and the rains that nourished the grass.

In winter, when the nights were cold, the Mongols thought they could see spirits dancing and leaping in the Gate of the Sky. These were the flaring lights that we call the northern lights.

At times Temujin would go alone to the top of a bare mountain to pray to this unseen power of the Sky. "Send the spirits of the upper air to befriend me," he prayed. "But here on earth send men to aid me."

From all the caravan roads hardened hunters,

solitary chieftains and cunning generals of war came to the Mongol Khan. They said of him: "He lets the hunter keep all the game he slays. After a battle, he gives each warrior a just share of the spoils. He dismounts from his horse to give it to one who needs it."

Temujin's ferocious fighters of the steppes gained a name for themselves—the *Kiyat,* or Raging Torrents. That was because they rushed over enemies like a swift torrent. It took an unbreakable will to manage them, but Temujin had such a will.

And he had a way of deciding wisely what each man could do. Borchu, for instance, was devoted but gentle. Temujin gave Borchu the place nearest him in council. To the brave but stupid Bowman he gave the privilege of carrying his own sword and quiver. Only those cunning in battle could be his commanders.

Such a man was Chepé, called the Arrow. He was a young warrior, originally of an enemy clan. When Temujin scattered the clan, his Mongol riders hunted down Chepé and surrounded him.

Chepé, on foot, called out that if they gave him a horse he would fight any one of them. Temujin granted his request. A swift, white-

Chepé cut his way through the Mongols and escaped.

nosed horse was led out to the young warrior. Chepé mounted it quickly, cut his way through the Mongols, and escaped. Later he rode back and said he was willing to serve the Khan who had given him the horse.

After a while Temujin made Chepé a *noyon*, or commander of a thousand. Long afterward when Chepé Noyon led an army to the west, he sent back a gift to the Mongol Khan. He sent a thousand white-nosed horses as a reminder that he had not forgotten how his life had been spared.

Even more cunning in battle was grim Subotai. Older than Chepé, he came in alone from the Reindeer People. "I will ward off your foes," Subotai promised Temujin, "as haircloth protects from the wind."

Subotai said little more, and Temujin waited to test him. Once when the Mongol horsemen were about to attack a Tartar encampment, the Khan asked for an officer to lead the first onset. Subotai rose and came forward. Pleased with his readiness, the Khan told him to pick a hundred chosen fighters to serve as his bodyguard.

But Subotai replied that he wanted no one to accompany him. Temujin then let him go alone.

Riding quietly into the Tartar camp, Subotai explained that he wanted to desert the Mongol Khan and to join them. He convinced them that the Mongol riders were far away, so the Tartars were utterly unprepared to resist when Temujin's horsemen dashed into the camp and scattered them.

Subotai had lied to deceive the Tartars, and he had risked his own life to save the lives of the Mongols. When he became a *noyon* like Chepé, he kept on doing the same thing—tricking the enemy and protecting his own men. He became known as Subotai the Invincible, because he won every battle no matter what the odds were against him.

"I was like a sleeping man," Temujin told his new champions, the Torrents, "when ye came to me. I was sitting in sadness aforetime when ye roused me."

By then Temujin was a grown man, with ten thousand wagon-tents to follow him. From a weak clan he had raised the Mongols of the Mountain of Power to a strong people.

But now he thought about making them even stronger. So long as he had enemies within the steppes, his people could not be safe. But what if he could unite all the warring nomads of the prairies and make himself their leader?

"The wise old men have always told us," he observed to the council, "that different hearts and minds cannot be in one body. But this I intend to bring about. I shall stretch my authority over all our neighbors."

6

The Magician of Death

As soon as Temujin set out to extend his authority, attempts were made to kill him. His enemies reasoned correctly that without Temujin's daring leadership the Yakka Mongols would not be dangerous.

Once they plotted to kill him by taking him into a tent where a hole had been dug under the carpet. Their behavior when they greeted him made Temujin suspicious, and he did not leave his guards to enter the tent.

But the most dangerous conspirator proved to be Tebtengri. This man was one of seven brothers, whose father had served Temujin's father, and he was also a shaman. Among the steppe-dwellers a shaman claimed to be more than a magician—he was known as a speaker-to-the-Sky-spirits. That is, he talked to the invisible spirits, very much like a medicine man of the American Indians.

Because the seven brothers came as friends of the Khan, Temujin had to welcome them to his encampments. Soon Tebtengri, jealous of the honor shown to the Mongol Khan, plotted to weaken him. His plan was not to attack him violently but rather to stir up quarrels that Temujin could not settle without causing more trouble.

First Tebtengri visited all the strongest chieftains who served Temujin and asked them why they obeyed a younger man so inferior to them. Meanwhile, Tebtengri's six brothers set upon the Bowman, the big brother of the Khan, and hurt him badly by pretending to wrestle with him. The Bowman complained to Temujin.

Now, as Khan of the Mongols, Temujin had to decide quarrels among his people fairly. If he favored his own kinsmen over others, his chieftains would realize he was not judging fairly. So he merely said to the Bowman, "You have boasted enough of your strength. Why do you let these fellows beat you?"

Tebtengri continued to go around the camps

stirring up trouble. Not knowing what to do, the angry Bowman stayed away from Temujin and kept to his own tent.

Then Tebtengri, the shaman, went to Temujin and said that he had been speaking with the spirits of the Sky. When a shaman did this he went into a trance. Tebtengri explained that during his trance he had flown on the wings of a great bird up into the Sky. "I heard this truth in the other world," Tebtengri told Temujin. *"For only a short while will Temujin rule his people. After that Kassar will rule. If you do not put an end to Kassar, your rule will soon end."*

Kassar was another name for the Bowman. Tebtengri seemed to be merely foretelling what would happen. Deceived by him, the Mongol Khan gave way to anger and rode to the tent where Kassar had been keeping himself. Probably in his rage he would have killed Kassar. But his mother heard what was happening and ran swiftly to the tent. Kneeling beside Kassar, she reminded Temujin how often his brother's arrows had saved his life. Mastering his anger, Temujin said, "I was frightened when I acted so. Now I am ashamed."

Next Tebtengri and his brothers tried to

shame Temugu, the youngest brother of the Khan. They forced the boy to kneel before them and beg them not to hurt him.

When Temujin heard about that, he began to realize how the shaman was working against him. But he could not prove that Tebtengri and his brothers had done any injury. By then they had gained quite a following among his people, who believed the shaman spoke with the voices of the spirit world. Moreover, it was the law of the Mongols—which Temujin enforced strictly —that no man should draw a weapon against another.

After the Khan had thought it all over, he decided he must get rid of Tebtengri without seeming to do so and without angering the people who had become the shaman's friends.

Temujin sent for his young brother Temugu and spoke to him. "I will summon Tebtengri to my *yurt* this day. Do with him as you please."

It was another law of the Mongols that no one could carry weapons into another's tent. When the wizard came, he had his six brothers and some officers with him. They all left their weapons outside the entrance of the tent, where Temujin sat alone by the hearth fire.

He greeted them and they seated themselves around him. Then Temugu entered and caught Tebtengri by the shoulders. "Yesterday," he said, "I was forced to kneel to you, but today I will try my strength with you."

For a while they struggled, and the wizard's friends rose to their feet.

"Do not wrestle here!" Temujin called to the two adversaries. "Go outside."

Outside the entrance three strong wrestlers

His back broken, Tebtengri lay motionless by the cart.

were waiting. Either Temujin or his brother had ordered them to wait there for this moment.

They seized Tebtengri as he came out, and broke his spine. The shaman lay motionless near the wheel of a cart.

"Look," cried Temugu. "Now when I want to try my strength with him he lies down and will not rise."

When the six brothers of the wizard looked out and saw Tebtengri's body, they shouted at Temujin, "O Khan, we have served you *until this day*. Now we are no longer your men."

They all made ready to rush upon the Mongol Khan. Temujin stood up.

He had no weapon and there was no way out of the *yurt* except by the entrance.

Sharply he spoke to the hostile clansmen. "Aside! I wish to go out."

Surprised by the unexpected command, they stepped back. Swiftly Temujin walked past them to his own guards.

He scarcely thought about the danger of that moment. But he feared that the death of the shaman might start a blood feud that would divide his people.

That night the red-headed Khan had his tent moved so it covered the body of Tebtengri. Then he ordered his trusted servants to lift the body out through the smoke hole so it would not be seen.

When crowds came the next day to look at the body, Temujin went out and told them, "Tebtengri plotted against my brothers. Now the spirits of Heaven have taken away both his life and his body."

So it seemed to the people that the wizard had been punished by the spirits of the Sky to whom he spoke. Some of the chieftains left Temujin in anger, but his wife, Bortay, remained faithfully at his side.

His fierce courage heartened his warriors. Yet he could not relax his watch for treachery. He was thirty years of age by then, and his sons rode on ponies at his side.

He let his oldest boy, Juchi, ride with Chepé Noyon, the Arrow Lord. The headstrong Chepé, who liked to clothe himself in sable boots and silvered chain mail, was happy only when off on an expedition. And Temujin allowed him to go with three other Torrents to aid the old Khan of the Keraits.

Temujin began to realize that he could never unite these warring peoples of the steppes unless he subdued them, one at a time. And it seemed as if he could never accomplish this as long as he had to fight to keep alive himself.

7

Great Hunt

WHEN JUCHI BECAME FIFTEEN YEARS OLD HE
was given the work of a grown man. Since he was
named "The Guest," he felt himself to be different from the other children. He used to quar-
rel with them and go off by himself.

Yet the stern Khan treated Juchi always as his
eldest son. And now he made Juchi Master of
the Hunting.

This was an important duty. Unlike the Euro-
pean nobles of that day, these nomad peoples
did not hunt for fun. Once or twice a year they
rounded up the wild game of the steppes to take
the meat of the animals, the fur or the hides, and
even the horns.

Wise, older men rode with Juchi when, as
Master of the Hunting, he made preparations

for his first drive on the wild animals. He had to travel hundreds of miles, crouched easily in the high saddle of the shaggy steppe ponies. These hardy beasts could amble along from dawn to dusk if the riders let them walk and graze at times. They could dig down with their hoofs through snow to get at the moss and withered grass beneath.

The first thing Juchi and the old hunters did was to find some natural barrier, like a line of steep hills with chalk cliffs. Then they galloped back thirty or forty miles and planted poles adorned with streamers in a vast half-circle facing the distant barrier.

Next, Juchi led out the clans of riders. Each regiment camped by the banner that marked its post. It was like going to war against all the wild animals. The riders carried their usual weapons, with the addition of large wicker shields.

When Temujin Khan rode up with his bodyguard and *noyons,* he gave a signal and the great hunt began. The warriors mounted and formed a close-knit line. With gongs sounding, drums beating and lance streamers flying, they surged forward, driving all wild life before them.

During this drive they were forbidden to use their weapons. They crushed through the undergrowth of ravines, climbed hillocks, and drove back the tigers, antelope or wolves that tried to slip through the line.

With each day the crush of driven animals became greater. At night the hunters lighted a circle of fires and posted sentries. Officers went the rounds as if before a battle.

If a panther tried to crawl between the fires, it had to be turned back unharmed. If a bear took refuge in a cave, it had to be brought out by ropes or poles without the use of a weapon.

This gave young boys many a chance to show their skill and fearlessness. In fact, it trained them to stalk and corner human enemies.

When the massed beasts felt themselves driven, the task became harder than ever. The horses of the hunters would not stand against a rush of wild boar. The men had to dismount and beat off the maddened tuskers.

When the party reached a river, most of the animals swam across. The hunters could not break their line to look for shallow fords. Instead, they urged the horses in, slipping from the saddles to hold onto the stirrup straps or manes. If the current was swift, they roped the horses together with lariats.

Guided by Juchi and the old hunters who had been over the ground before, the human half-circle narrowed, closing in against the barrier of the steep cliffs. Within this circle where drums and gongs resounded, deer with quivering flanks leaped into view, and the tawny shadows of tigers slipped through the brush.

Then the hunt came to rest. Temujin, the Khan, rode first into the milling animals. Now he could use his weapons, and he rushed in, slashing at a leaping panther with his sword, or transfixing swift antelope with his arrows. Then he withdrew to a hilltop and watched under a pavilion.

Other chieftains and officers took their turns killing the game. Each man remembered which animals he had struck down. After the young boys had tested their skill, Temujin's smaller children came to him, as custom required, to beg that the surviving animals be allowed to escape.

He granted their request, and then all the people turned to gathering up the carcasses.

Juchi was eager and fearless in carrying out

his new task as Master of the Hunting. Yet he had one failing. He did not like to take orders from others—perhaps because he went off alone so much. And Temujin, as you have seen, insisted that every order be carried out to the end.

Moreover, Juchi seemed to have bad luck in doing things. He was directing one of his first hunts when disaster befell the Mongols and Temujin suffered his worst defeat.

The hunt over the prairies had barely begun. As usual the Mongols sent out scouts in all directions to watch for any sign of the approach of foemen.

One day some of the scouts failed to return. No particular notice was taken of their long absence, because they might have lingered to watch a passing caravan, or have camped out for the night. But after the fires were lighted along the hunting circle that night, two unknown herdsmen galloped in asking for the Khan of the Mongols. They brought terrible news.

From under the setting sun, they said, great clans were moving with unfamiliar banners. These strange foemen were advancing to catch the Mongols scattered in their hunting. And the leaders of these allied clans were the Keraits, who had been Temujin's only fast friends.

These foemen had captured some of the Mongol scouts. No one tried to blame Juchi for this misfortune, because the scouts had been sent out by the military officers, not by him. Yet it had happened while he was directing the march.

The news the herdsmen brought meant one thing to Temujin: The alliance of the nomads he had hoped to form and rule had been made by his enemies and was being turned against him. His particular friends, the Christian Keraits, now led the attack against him. And now in spite of his wariness he had been caught unprepared to fight.

In that last misfortune, too, Juchi unwittingly played a part. To understand why Temujin was unprepared, it is necessary to know what had happened before this particular hunt.

For a long time Temujin had aided Toghrul Khan of the Keraits, and had besought the shrewd old chieftain to come under his protection.

Then luck seemed to help his plan. For the Golden Emperor, who ruled behind the Great Wall in Cathay, had sent an army into the steppes to punish the nearest nomads. These happened to be the Tartars of the Buyar Lake. Temujin had seized the chance to interfere.

When the Tartars retreated before the army of the Cathayans—mostly foot soldiers who could not catch the Tartar horsemen—Temujin and the Keraits had fallen on the Tartars, broken their strength, and forced them to submit to Temujin.

This victory had made his powerful enemies suspicious. Over the grasslands couriers galloped with the word that Temujin sought to make himself master of all the steppe people. The Kerait commanders did not like it.

Their prince, the son of Toghrul, was afraid of Temujin's influence with his father. He went to Jamuka, the cunning chieftain of the western clans—the Turkish folk, the Naimans and others of the caravan roads.

Jamuka, a kinsman of Temujin, wanted the khanship of the Yakka Mongols for himself. So he and Toghrul's son decided to destroy Temujin by a trick. They persuaded Toghrul

Khan to renew his friendship with the Mongol by offering to give a princess of the Keraits in marriage to Juchi.

Temujin distrusted the messengers, but he could not refuse the marriage offer. So he was traveling west that spring to take Juchi to his bride, and to take some of the game they killed as a gift to the old Toghrul. (The Kerait chieftain was still the leading figure of the nomad clans; the Chinese people of Cathay called him Wang Khan, or Lord King.)

Thus, the Mongols were unprepared for war as they traveled west, hunting on the way. The wily Jamuka had tricked Temujin, and the Mongols were caught in a trap.

On the night the Mongols learned that foemen were advancing on them, the boy Juchi sat, tense, on a corner of the white horsehide at the feet of the Khan.

One by one the *noyons* and commanders stepped in through the entrance of the wide *yurt* and knelt in a ring around the Khan. They folded their scarred hands in their long leather sleeves and lifted bronzed faces to the torchlight.

Chepé Noyon, the impetuous, sat silent. Muhuli, the aged, fingered the beads of a rosary. Subotai breathed deeply, winded from a headlong ride through the sleeping *yurts*. Guïldar, keeper of the standard, stood impassive by the wine table where he could watch the entrance, for he was on guard duty. Juchi listened, unspeaking, to the *kouriltai,* the council of the leaders.

Temujin motioned them to speak, one by one. His head, under its mantle of white felt, was thrust out from his stooped shoulders. His gray-green eyes gleamed in the torchlight.

One by one, he echoed their words. When the Khan spoke, the words became commands. Officers rose and went out to obey them.

Juchi heard them, like strokes of doom: Let the guards of the Khan's tent go among the *yurts,* rouse the sleepers . . . send the boys to stampede and scatter the herds . . . leave the *yurts,* the ox-wagons and camel carts standing, they cannot be taken . . . mount all women and children with small chests of their most valuable things . . . take all weapons . . . flee swiftly toward the sunrise . . . keep the campfires burning high to deceive enemy scouts. . . .

The Mongol commanders knelt around the Khan.

Most of the herds and possessions and all the wagons would be lost. The Mongol regiments would hold the rear of the flight. They would make a stand only in the gorge beyond the last river, after sunrise. . . .

In the drifting dust of the sunset that followed, Juchi watched their terrible defeat. The valley where they struggled seemed to be alive with hordes of the enemy. The Mongols were too few to check them.

Unnoticed, Juchi followed behind the stirrup of Temujin. They went back and back, through the dust.

There seemed to be no way to stop the retreat. Suddenly Temujin turned to glance at the sinking sun. Then he reined toward the standard pole with its nine white yak tails.

Guïldar waited by the pole with the remainder of the Khan's household guard. Reaching him, Temujin ordered him to take these guards and the standard and break through the ranks of the Keraits—to circle them and plant the standard on the hill to the left behind them.

"Ay, my brother," replied the weary Guïldar. "I will break through all who oppose me. I will take your standard to the hill. If I fall, do you nourish and rear my children."

It seemed to Juchi to be a move of desperation, this attempt to break through the Keraits and their allies, who were victorious everywhere. But the mighty Guïldar did break through. He planted the Mongol standard high on the hill and held it.

The sun was just setting. The Keraits fancied they were being attacked by fresh warriors, and they hung back. When the sun set, they withdrew a little to find out what was happening.

This enabled Temujin to bring Guïldar back, and to flee to the east with the remainder of his horsemen. He had kept himself and the nucleus of his clan alive.

During the retreat he summoned Juchi and told him to begin again the great hunt of wild game. Now they had more need than before of the wild flesh and hides.

"We have fought," said Toghrul Khan to Jamuka and his allies, "a man with whom we should never have quarreled."

8

Lord of High Asia

SOMETIMES WHEN A MAN SHOWS THAT HE IS
able to stand firm against misfortune, others
come to him for help. That happened now to the
stubborn Mongol Khan.

Other chieftains of clans east of Lake Baikul
became afraid of the supremacy of Toghrul, or
Wang Khan, with his Keraits and armies of the
west. They sent to Temujin for advice—or to discover what he meant to do next.

And he called them into a great council, to decide what *they* meant to do next. Some of them
wanted to submit to Wang Khan and Jamuka.
But others wanted to accept Temujin's leadership in the crisis. These last prevailed.

"From the beginning I told you these lands
must have one master," Temujin said to them
bitterly. "You would not understand. Now,

when you fear that Wang Khan will treat you as
he has treated me, you have chosen me to be
your leader. Well, I will keep these lands of our
ancestors safe for you."

Once he had accepted the leadership of the
eastern clans, Temujin did not waste one
month in delay. He knew that his only chance of
victory was to strike at the western peoples before they could gather again into a single horde
at the beginning of the summer. He rode west
around Lake Baikul with his new forces before
snow left the valleys.

Like a storm sweeping across the steppes, the
Mongol horde struck its enemies in their home
towns and grazing lands.

It galloped over the unprepared Keraits.
Temujin did not linger even to count up the captured wealth of this rich people—the saddles
covered with silk, the fine steel swords, and
goblets of silver. But he did stop long enough to
give the pavilion of Wang Khan, hung with
cloth-of-gold, to the two herdsmen who had
warned him of the coming of the Keraits during
his hunt.

When he overtook the mass of the Kerait
horsemen, he surrounded them with his war-

riors and offered them their lives if they would serve him. "You have fought like heroes to save your lord," he told them. "Now join with my warriors and serve me."

More than the rich spoil of the encampments, he valued this manpower that he could use. The surviving Keraits joined his banners.

But the Mongol Khan was savage in his pursuit of the enemy commanders. Wang Khan fled hopelessly with his son far to the west, where both were killed by Turkish tribesmen. Jamuka, who had plotted to destroy Temujin, was captured alive.

"What fate do you expect?" Temujin asked him.

"The same that I would have given you," responded Jamuka without hesitation. "The slow death."

He meant the Chinese torture of slow dismemberment, which begins the first day with cutting off the joints of the little fingers, and continues with the slicing up of all the limbs. Temujin, however, followed the custom of his own people, which forbade shedding the blood of a chieftain of royal birth. Jamuka was led away to be smothered under heavy cloths.

By conquering the Keraits, Temujin had gained for himself cities and plowed lands along the caravan tracks. Most of the conquerors of the Gobi before his time would have been content with that. But the inflexible Mongol Khan led his horde on to the west—up the valleys of the Naimans, to crush the last of the tribal peoples in arms against him.

A thousand miles he had come from the Great Wall of Cathay. Another four hundred he sent his commanders, from the long white mountains of the north, over the deserts, into the Five Cities of the western Uighurs, a Turkish people of high culture. Among these Uighurs his officers noticed dignified figures in robes. These were not warriors, but merchants, astronomers, and physicians. They were strange to the barbaric Mongols, who sent them, captive, to Temujin.

A bearded Uighur was brought before him, holding fast to a small gold object curiously made.

"Why do you cling to this thing?" the Mongol asked.

"I wish to care for it until the death of him who entrusted it to me."

The bearded man held a golden seal in his hand.

"You are a loyal servant," the Khan admitted, "but your master is dead and all he possessed is now mine. Tell me what this token is good for."

The captive, a minister of the Uighur court, explained that the gold object was a seal. It was used to stamp any written command, as proof that his royal master had given the command.

Promptly Temujin ordered a seal like it to be made for himself. He pardoned the captive Uighur, keeping him to teach Juchi and his other sons the writing of that people—a writing that they probably had learned from wandering Christian priests long before. Although Temujin himself could not write, he realized quickly enough that wisdom as well as accounts could be kept stored up in books.

He was also wise enough not to interfere with the priests he found along the caravan roads—whether Buddhist lamas, or Moslems, or Nestorian Christians who had ventured so far into Asia. The Mongol shamans had great influence with his own people, so he expected these priests could aid him in managing the different people of the west.

For five years the Mongol Khan led this sweep of his horsemen around the sands of the Gobi. The wild folk—the Mongols, Turks, and tundra people of high Asia—were in awe of the leader who wielded such power.

Because he forbade feuds, they ceased. Because of his encouragement, great caravans moved safely over the trails from the heights of the lofty Th'ian Shan to the Great Wall.

Those officers who had served him best—and Chepé Noyon and Subotai were first among them—he honored and raised above their fellows. Remembering that they had gained his victories, he made them *tarkhans.* This meant they could choose lands for themselves where they wished, and take their pick of the captives. They were freed from all taxation and punishment—even the death penalty would be spared them.

Temujin called his new *tarkhans,* along with the chieftains of the nomad peoples, to a council. It was held on a river north of their new prairie city of clay and thatch houses called Karakorum, or Black Sands.

There, when the council sat in the smoke of the campfires, the Mongol Khan asked them to select one man to rule them all. Only in that way could they hold together.

The council hailed him as leader. A soothsayer came forward to urge that with his new authority he should have a new name, *Genghis Khan.* That meant Great Khan, or Khan-to-the-Sea.

For Temujin, now Genghis Khan, had accomplished what the wise old men had said could never be done. He had united under one mind and heart all the nomad peoples from the mountains of inner Asia to the sea.

9

Breaking the Great Wall

IT WAS THE BEGINNING OF THE THIRTEENTH
century then—the year 1206 of our calendar.

Genghis Khan, as they called Temujin there-
after, went up again to the top of the great
Mountain of Power to pray and think about
what he should do next.

Most of the nomad people told themselves
that their new master, Genghis Khan, must be
aided by the power of Heaven. What he thought
about that we do not know. Being an ignorant
tribesman, he probably believed that if he
wanted anything he had to contrive to get it for
himself.

Until then he had just about managed to sur-
vive with his people. But even when they were
all gathered together, the nomad folk were

poor, with few weapons and comforts. Like their ancestors long before them, they still lived on their herds.

Yet they were a proud people. If you had managed to live with your horse, hunting on great plains somewhere, you would be somewhat proud of your skill, even if you had very few possessions to show for it. You would probably look down on people far off who shut themselves up in warm houses and merely bought what they needed at stores. At the same time you might want very much to be able to go to school as they could and to take home things you saw in store windows, although you had no money to pay for such things.

Well, something like that was going on in the mind of Genghis Khan.

While his people still lived as their ignorant ancestors had, all around them civilized folk had been making inventions and building walled cities to protect themselves. From these wealthy empires of the outer world, caravans brought in the steel weapons, fine silk, and life-giving wheat that the nomads craved.

As he had said long before, Genghis Khan was not a merchant able to buy such luxuries. But now he was strong enough to ride into the outer world and just take them.

When he came down from the Mountain of Power that year, he stood beneath the old standard of his *yurt*—the same one that Guïldar had carried—and spoke to all the chieftains who were now his officers:

"Those men who will share with me the good and the bad of the future, whose loyalty will be like the clear rock crystal—I wish them to be called Mongols. Above everything that breathes on earth I wish them to be raised to power."

That seemed impossible to accomplish. But up to now Temujin-Genghis Khan had managed somehow to make good all his promises.

"An action is only good," he told Juchi, who was now a young man, "if you carry it out to the end."

So at the start he joined all the wild folk of the steppes into a single gigantic clan which he called the Mongols. Thus, the Mongols included the wise and mysterious Uighurs, the stalwart Keraits, the hardy Yakka Mongols, the ferocious Tartars and the dour Merkits, together with the reindeer keepers and hunters of the tundras.

Before his time other conquerors had banded

together these nomads of the Gobi, but no one had ever held over them the inflexible authority of Genghis Khan.

His name was written down by his new secretaries in letters of gold.

His Law held fast on every human being and animal. For instance, anyone who stole an animal was put to death, after he confessed. A warrior who left his squad of ten during a battle suffered the same penalty.

The Mongol riders did not turn aside now to gather up loot because they knew that all the spoil would be dealt out fairly to everyone.

And the commands of the new lord of high Asia were carried from encampment to encampment by riders on the swiftest horses. Changing to fresh ponies at each stopping place, these couriers who carried the orders of the Great Khan in sealed tubes of gold would cover two hundred miles in a single day. They greased their faces and bodies to endure the terrible cold of winter. Bells jingled from their belts to warn other travelers to clear the road for them.

In this way they made even faster time than the riders of the American Pony Express more than six hundred years later.

During the winter snow they went on great hunts.

Genghis Khan did not allow other men to stay long out of the saddle, either. Instead of letting them rest during the winter snow, he ordered them out on great hunts, like the one Juchi had directed. And when grass came in the spring, his couriers summoned all commanders to the Khan's council. "He who does not come," said Genghis Khan grimly, "will disappear. He will be lost forever like an arrow shot far into reeds."

He gave some of his new commanders, like Subotai, practice in invading a country. Sending them beyond the sandy Gobi, he bade them punish the outlaw kingdom of Hsia, where the people thought themselves safe among their hills.

These Mongol commanders brought back captured herds, and orphaned children to be adopted by Mongol women. They brought back weapons and useful spoil in ox-carts. Men who resisted them were killed. Very soon the sight of Mongol banners over the hard-riding horsemen was enough to cause terror in a country.

Now Genghis Khan was careful to lend other divisions—one of them commanded by Chepé Noyon—to the great Golden Emperor of Cathay.

Cathay, which is what China was called then, was upset by civil war, as China has been lately. The Kin, or Golden Emperor, of the north fought with the Sung Emperor of the south.

The Mongols lent by Genghis Khan helped the Golden Emperor. And Chepé Noyon and the others took careful notice of all the rich country within the Great Wall. When they rode back to the horde in the Gobi, they told of the wonders they had seen: roads that ran clear across the rivers on stone bridges; wooden *kibitkas* floating in the rivers; rich folk who went about in chairs carried by barefoot slaves, with parasols held over them to protect them from the sun. It was all very wonderful!

Chepé Noyon and the others begged Genghis Khan to loose them against Cathay. They were sure they could conquer it for him.

But the stern Khan would let them try no such thing. He knew, from their tales, that Cathay had *millions* of people—most of them pent up in cities with walls as high as the trees of the Mountain of Power. To defend these walls they had huge armies with machines that cast stones and the fearsome Fire that Flies.

It would have been disastrous to lead his eager horsemen armed with bows and lances against such walls. But all this time, although he seemed to be waiting quietly in his desert town of Karakorum, Genghis Khan was learning more and more about the strength and weakness of mighty Cathay.

From time to time he let his regiments parade along the outside of the first barrier, the

Great Wall that ran over plains and hills with towers to defend its gates.

The guards on duty upon the Wall got accustomed to watching these Mongols riding harmlessly by. And then suddenly Genghis Khan ordered his regiments to break through one of the gates.

He was inside the Great Wall.

Still, the Cathayans did not feel the danger closing in on them. Instead of attacking them, the Mongol Khan led his army aside to invade the barbaric coastal people of Liao-tung—the Iron people. And they were more enemies than friends of the Golden Emperor.

Yet Genghis Khan was making his way, without seeming to do so, into Cathay.

10

The Man of Wisdom

GENGHIS KHAN RODE WITHIN SIGHT OF YEN-KING, the Great Court itself. This was the city of the Golden Emperor, called Peiping today. For the first time he beheld the stupendous walls stretching around the hills and waterways that guarded the citadel of Cathay. Then he moved on without doing any harm except seizing forage and food.

It was like the seemingly peaceful parade of the banners outside the Great Wall.

Up by the sea, however, Chepé Noyon was besieging a strong city called Liao-yang, held by the Cathayans.

The impetuous Chepé was not making much progress. His horsemen could not climb the sheer walls. He had no engines with which to break down the walls. And the garrison refused to come out from the shelter of its brick ramparts.

So the Mongols tried a trick. They left their tents, carts and baggage, and rode off with their herds as if giving up the siege.

For two days the Mongols rode away slowly. Then they shifted to their fastest horses and galloped back in a single night. The garrison of Liao-yang had no Pony Express to warn them that the Mongols were coming back.

These soldiers of Liao-yang were occupied in plundering the Mongols' abandoned baggage and carrying it inside the walls. All gates were left open, and townspeople mingled with the soldiers.

At daybreak the Mongols rode in upon them —and straight on through the open gates into the city. The Cathayan garrison was massacred.

Chepé Noyon got the city and rescued all his baggage as well.

Each year Genghis Khan was discovering more about mighty Cathay. He found out that the Golden Emperor, although called the Son of Heaven, lived shut up in his palaces. His court, although called the Clouds of Heaven, occupied itself in seeking pleasure and gaining wealth. The millions of people in Cathay were all divided up into slaves and peasants, beggars and students, mandarins, dukes and soldiers. All these different classes believed the Golden Emperor, Wai Wang, to be supremely powerful.

Genghis Khan thought otherwise. "The Son of Heaven," he announced, "should be an extraordinary man, but this Wai Wang is an imbecile, unworthy of a throne."

He had sent a message to Wai Wang himself. It did not sound at all like a message from an ignorant nomad chieftain to a great and all-powerful emperor. "My dominion is now so well arranged," said the Mongol, "that I can go to Cathay. Is the Golden Emperor ready to receive us? We will come with an army that is like a roaring ocean, and we will stay until we are victorious or defeated."

Genghis Khan had an army of only about a hundred and fifty thousand horsemen with which to attack a dozen huge walled cities filled with many millions of people. Why did he tell Wai Wang so plainly what he meant to do?

For one thing the shrewd Mongol had learned from the Cathayans themselves how to deal with those walls. For another thing, he wanted to make the unwarlike Wai Wang and the millions of Cathayans afraid.

So in this year of 1214 he led his horde against Cathay to inspire fear.

Spies went ahead. Scouts followed along all the roads. Then the hard-riding Mongol horsemen came in four armies, not just one. Juchi led a division around through Liao-tung.

These armies ravaged the countryside, driving hosts of captives along with them; they encircled and cut off the Cathayan armies on the roads. By doing all this they appeared many times as strong as they really were.

And, secluded in his citadel at Yen-king, surrounded by his slaves and singing girls, the Golden Emperor became afraid. He, Wai Wang, made no move to protect his people. So a band of his nobles pulled him from the throne and killed him. They named another, Hsüan Tsung, emperor in his place.

But Hsüan Tsung did not have courage enough to stay in Yen-king. In spite of the protest of his ministers, he fled to the south.

Wai Wang was surrounded by slaves and singing girls.

That was exactly what Genghis Khan wanted to happen. For when their new emperor deserted them, the people of Cathay did not know who would protect them. So they too became afraid.

11

End of an Empire

THE MONGOLS GAVE THE CATHAYANS NO TIME to regain their courage.

The horsemen of the Gobi trampled down growing crops; they burned villages like torches along their line of march. When their horned standards showed on the skyline, people fled wailing.

There was no emperor to protect them now. The power of the Mongol Khan pursued them unchecked.

Genghis Khan kept on taunting the fugitive Hsüan Tsung. Years before, the Emperor had demanded a yearly tribute from the nomad clans of the Gobi. Now Genghis Khan sent a message demanding tribute from the Emperor himself. And the unhappy Hsüan Tsung, hoping to get a truce, sent hundreds of young slaves with fine horses and cartloads of gold and silk. He did not get the truce.

After that, some of the Cathayan generals deserted him to join Genghis Khan, who, although a barbarian, was a real soldier.

By then the Mongol armies were capturing the strongest cities. They promised to spare the lives of the city dwellers if the gates were opened to them. When the Cathayan troops defended the walls, the Mongols built huge inclines of earth piled as high as the parapets of the walls. Then they attacked up the slanting earth.

Sometimes they drove crowds of captives ahead of them against the walls, and the Cathayans surrendered rather than kill the prisoners who were their own countrymen.

When a city tried to defend itself, the Mongols got into it somehow and slaughtered all human beings except skilled engineers, physicians and teachers. These they drove off to serve them, with all the cattle and sheep. Then they burned the houses and pulled down standing walls.

Often there was nothing left of such a city except piles of dirt, where grass grew to feed the animals.

The Mongols wanted to leave nothing behind that could resist them in Cathay.

Meanwhile, some of the faithful generals of the empire discovered how few the nomads really were. They had noticed too that the Mongol horses became weak and tired, especially in winter. These Cathayan commanders defended themselves bravely, and besought the Emperor to gather one great army to sweep the Mongols out of the land.

Hsüan Tsung had treasure enough and men enough to do that. But before he could try anything of the kind, he heard something that terrified him.

Mongol horsemen were riding furiously after him. A single division had been sent by Genghis Khan to hunt Hsüan Tsung as if he were an animal. The timid Emperor gathered together his women and mandarins, as well as all his jewels and gold, and hurried farther south.

The pursuing Mongols gained on him. They did not stop to rest or to loot, but kept on tracking him. With this peril at his heels, Hsüan

Tsung fled to the Yellow River, to take refuge near his old enemies, the Sung.

There was no chance now of his returning to Cathay.

Genghis Khan had gained the victory over the Golden Emperor. And from that moment he wasted no more thought on the unfortunate Hsüan Tsung.

He called in his armies to rest. Subotai came in announcing the submission of Korea. Chepé Noyon was sent back to Karakorum in the Gobi to take care of matters there. The governing of the conquered lands of north China was turned over to Muhuli and the princes of Liao, the foes of the Cathayans.

For Genghis Khan knew that educated men could collect treasure and set the disordered inhabitants to work again better than he could himself. Probably a captive prince, Ye Liu Kutsai, convinced him of that.

All this time Genghis Khan had made no attempt to capture the stronghold of Cathay, Yenking itself. But now, with its emperor gone and its armies scattered, the great city remained alone, without hope of aid.

Understanding this, the Mongol Khan did not trouble to ride against Yen-king himself. "Walls," he said to those near him, "are no stronger than the men who defend them."

So he sent Subotai with no more than five thousand riders, and Mingan, a prince of Liao-tung, to manage for him. They camped around Yen-king, keeping food from reaching the city.

Above them loomed the citadel with its pleasure lake and pine-covered hills, and its massive walls within walls. Yet the soldiers within it had no leaders and they quarreled among themselves. When Subotai's horsemen appeared in the suburbs, some of the soldiers marched out to join him.

Imperial women of Cathay who tried to escape from the starving palace lost their way in the disordered streets. Cathayan soldiers broke into the stores to loot, and soon fires sprang up in different parts of the city. No one tried to put out the fires.

Up in the palace eunuchs and slaves hurried through the corridors, their arms filled with stolen jeweled ornaments.

The imperial hall of audience was deserted,

because the sentries left to join the looters. In his chamber, the Cathayan general who commanded the palace watched the mobs and the conflagration. He remained at his post, but he could do nothing more.

On the table lay the last decree of his master, Hsüan Tsung. It was a hurried message, pardoning all criminals in Cathay and promising rich gifts to the soldiers who would fight for Hsüan Tsung.

This surviving general read the decree again. Then he sat down and wrote a message of his own. He wrote that he deserved death because he had not been able to defend Yen-king, which had been given to him to command. After that he divided his own clothes and belongings among his servants and dismissed them from the room.

When he was alone, he drank a cup of poison. He died at his post, a braver man than the emperor he served.

The Mongols rode in, through burning streets and terrified crowds, to a deserted palace.

Among the captives brought before Genghis

Khan was a tall young prince of Liao-tung who had served the Cathayans. His deep, clear voice attracted the attention of the Khan.

"Why did you stay with the dynasty that was the old enemy of your family?" the Mongol asked curiously.

"My father was a servant of the Golden Emperor. I could not do otherwise than he did."

This reply pleased Genghis Khan. He asked the young prince's name and learned that it was Ye Liu Kutsai. "Since you served your former master so well, you can serve me with trust," he observed. "Be one among my followers."

When he was alone, he drank a cup of poison.

Now the bold Ye Liu Kutsai was a philosopher, a man of wisdom. Genghis Khan soon learned that this young scholar could tell him about medicine to cure sickness, and explain the mysterious movements of the stars in the night sky.

And Ye Liu Kutsai had the courage to tell the awe-inspiring Mongol the truth. Many times he shielded a conquered people from the anger of the Great Khan. "You have conquered an empire in the saddle," he warned his master once, "but you cannot govern it so."

When the Mongol officers jeered at him, asking him what he, a man of books, hoped to do among a fellowship of warriors, this wise prince did not become frightened or lose his temper. "To use your bows," he told them, "you first call upon a maker of arrows. To learn wisdom you have need of a maker of books."

Genghis Khan himself realized the truth of that. He was using these learned Cathayan captives to discover how bridges could be built and walls destroyed.

12

Throne of the Black Sands

WHAT WOULD GENGHIS KHAN DO NEXT? IN ALL vast Asia people were asking themselves that question.

In his desert city of Karakorum—Black Sands —he had gathered together everything that a nomad chieftain could desire. His herds covered the prairies, the black *yurts* of his clans stretched to the skyline.

No longer did he have enemies near by to look out for. Chepé Noyon had attended to that.

While Genghis Khan had been conquering Cathay, another chieftain had tried to seize his power in the western mountains, known as Black Cathay. And Chepé Noyon had been sent to punish this master of Black Cathay.

Through the mountains the Arrow Lord had

raced with his horsemen. He sent back to Karakorum the head of the rebellious Khan of Black Cathay. At the same time he sent to Genghis Khan a gift of a thousand white-nosed horses. As mentioned earlier, these were sent as a reminder that Chepé had not forgotten how the Khan had spared his life many years before.

"Do not become too proud because of your success," the great Mongol warned his lieutenant.

There was little danger of that. Wherever the Khan's couriers galloped, from the Pacific Ocean to Tibet, his commands were obeyed.

No longer did he sit in a domed leather *yurt*. His lofty pavilion of white felt was lined with silk. By the entrance stood a silver table set with mare's milk, fruit and meat, so that all who came to him could eat as much as they wished.

Kneeling by his feet, Bortay and the other women wore velvet gowns covered with strings of pearls. Juchi and the three other sons of Bortay wore the long padded robes of Cathay, with feathers hanging from their hats.

Behind the Khan, scribes of Cathay waited to write down his words.

Only Genghis Khan himself **was** unchanged

in his dress. He still clothed himself in the leather and fur of his early years. The thin mustache on his bony, lined face had turned gray. His narrowed eyes gleamed as watchfully as when he had strained for the sight of a horseman moving on the skyline.

He had kept his promise to his steppe nomads. All around his desert city stood granaries of rice, millet and wheat—food enough for men and beasts. Mongol accounts say that carts of gold and silver stood near by without any guards to watch over them. So utterly was the Law of Genghis Khan—which forbade stealing —obeyed.

Because of that Law, peace prevailed for thousands of miles around him. No one could go to war unless the Khan himself ordered it.

But the victorious Mongol had promised his people more than that. He had said he would raise them over all others who breathed in the world.

Once he asked a *tarkhan* attending him what could bring the greatest happiness to a man.

The officer thought a moment and said, "A swift horse to ride over the grasslands, and a falcon on your wrist to fly after game."

"No," responded the Khan, "to crush your enemies, and see them fall at your feet—to take their horses and belongings, and hear the lamentation of their women. That is best."

He felt the scars of many wounds in his body. In all his fifty-four years he had known only merciless warfare. Probably in spite of his victories, he felt that he had one more thing to accomplish.

It was something no one else had accomplished. For years while he rode with his horde he had been planning it out in his mind. Remember that he had told Juchi an action was good only if you followed it out to the end.

Remember, too, that Genghis Khan was still a barbarian. He did not care anything for civilization, with its money and crowded cities. Without it he had managed to do well enough.

His final plan was to strip everything useful from the outlying civilizations. All the gold, the fine cloth, and especially the weapons would be brought in by caravan to Karakorum.

So would young children and older captives with skilled minds—philosophers and engineers and others—be brought in to serve the Mongols.

Meanwhile, his military commanders would

keep order in the outlying empires, as they were doing now in Korea and north China. After a time there would be no great cities or fortifications left in the surrounding civilized countries to resist the Mongol armies.

Then the family of Genghis Khan would rule most of Asia from their home in the steppes. Already, because their names had been written in gold ink, his family was known as the *Altyn Uruk,* or Golden Family.

His sons would direct the military commanders, meeting with them each year at the great council.

Under these commanders, his people—all those called Mongols of the Gobi Desert— would be supreme over other captive peoples.

By this plan Genghis Khan would transform his part of the world into a vast grazing ground. Here captive human beings would work like animals to carry out his needs.

In fact, the strange skill of the Mongols in managing throngs of people came from their long experience in herding animals.

This was a terrifying plan of the nomad conqueror's. Still he managed to carry it all out, except for one thing, which was not his fault. For he could not guess that his sons would not grow up to be like himself. Yet he did seem to have some misgivings, for he said once, "My descendants will clothe themselves in cloth-of-gold, and hold the fairest women in their arms. They will ride about in luxury, and they will forget to whom they owe all those things."

To Juchi and the other three sons of Bortay he gave learned tutors like Ye Liu Kutsai. He wanted them to be skilled in the wisdom of books, an advantage he had never possessed.

But Juchi, in spite of his duty as Master of the Hunting, was content only when he was leading some expedition far away. Once he found his way through the barrier of the mountain ranges of mid-Asia. Beyond them he discovered quietly flowing rivers and fertile steppes, like the homeland of the Mongols.

The Chinese professors called this new land *Ta-tsin,* the Far West. It was really part of the steppes of what we call Russia. Juchi longed to make it his home but duty called him back to the Mongol horde.

In another way, Genghis Khan himself learned about another part of the world, to the southwest.

There, beyond the mountain ranges, lay valleys where snow never fell, watered by rivers that never froze. There were gardens always green.

Merchants who thronged now to Karakorum, bringing the goods of the outer world, told him about the garden city of Samarkand, and Baghdad, ruled by the Caliph. They showed him swords of Damascus steel that he could bend like a whip in his hands. These Moslem merchants of the caravans made him gifts of carved ivory and shining brocade, carpets and silver lamps—wealth that Genghis Khan had never known.

Never did he bargain with the strange caravan masters. The Mongols had not learned to pay for things. They simply took everything, as a gift to the Khan, and then gave back to the merchants bars of silver or gold or other things. And often the men of the caravans made fortunes in a single journey.

All this time, however, Genghis Khan and his commanders were finding out from the merchants where the mountains could be crossed, where the roads led to the new world of the southwest, and when the grass was good for grazing there. After a while the Mongols sent merchants of their own to spy out the roads that armies could follow.

Genghis Khan was very curious about this sun-warmed west filled with mosques, or Moslem churches, and palaces.

Then unexpectedly he received a message from the far-off Caliph of Baghdad. Something of the fame of Genghis Khan had been told, perhaps by his own merchants, to the mysterious Caliph. The message was secret, because it had been written in dyed ink on the shaven head of

The secret message was written on his shaven head.

a pilgrim, whose hair had been allowed to grow over it.

When this pilgrim's head was shaved again, the message could be read. The Mongols had gathered around them scholars of many lands who could read different kinds of writing.

The Caliph of Baghdad appealed to the Great Khan for aid against another ruler, Muhammad Shah, who was trying to make him a prisoner. At least this is what he said.

This appeal did not please Genghis Khan, although he understood that the Caliph was a kind of Moslem high priest, and he had a habit of protecting priests. He thought this Caliph must be a weak prince, to send a message so secretly. But he sent Mongol envoys to the far-off Shah to find out about the situation and especially to open trade with cities like Samarkand.

Muhammad Shah proved to be both proud and arrogant. He had a habit of putting to death people who offended him. He put the Mongol envoys to death.

Now in the eyes of the Khan, an envoy was safe from harm. Remembering the appeal of the Caliph, he decided to march with all the horde, veterans of Cathay, against the wealthy Shah.

Yet he was careful to send a warning ahead. "You will have war. What will happen then, we do not know. Only God knows."

The first thing that happened was that the Mongols started to march very early in the autumn, and as soon as they got to their saddles snow began to fall around them. This untimely snowfall worried the Mongol Khan, who thought it might be a sign from the Sky that he should not go on the campaign.

So he summoned the man of wisdom, Ye Liu Kutsai, to explain it to him. The quick-witted Cathayan, who wanted the Mongol horde to go as far away as possible from China, made this answer: "It is a sign from Heaven that the monarch of the cold north will conquer the lord of the sunny south."

This satisfied Genghis Khan, and the drums sounded to start the march.

13

Over the Roof of the World

THE ROUTE TO SAMARKAND WAS NOT AT ALL like the level road into Cathay. It led the Mongols far off, over deserts without water, through mountain ranges where the only pass was the Gate of the Winds. Then it climbed up to ice-covered heights that the nomads called the Roof of the World.

Caravans had made this journey. But the loads of the caravans were carried by camels through the sandy wastes, and by sturdy yaks over the snow and ice passes, and then by horses on the far grasslands. And the Mongols were an army, venturing where no army had been able to go before.

Perhaps even Genghis Khan did not really want to leave his prairies to make this journey.

Once, when he passed a hill covered with a dense forest, he drew rein and sat in the saddle to look at it.

"A good place for deer, and for hunting," he said. "A good resting place for an old man."

Then he went on. Ye Liu Kutsai had warned him that he could not govern his empire from the saddle, but Genghis Khan trusted that the commands he sent back by courier over the post roads would be obeyed.

His Mongol horde got across the dry lands. Spare herds, water and fodder had been collected carefully along the line of their march. When winter set in, snow gave them water enough.

Their heavy felt capes protected them in storms. At need they took shelter from the wind and cold in their leather-domed *yurts*.

So they climbed the dark ravines, the Gate of the Winds.

All the riders carried dried food—smoke-cured meat, and milk curds that could be dissolved in water. They also had lengths of light strong rope which they attached to carts to help pull the loads. They had spare ponies to which they could shift to rest their own mounts. They had short axes with which to fell trees to make bridges over rushing ice rivers and ravines.

Chinese engineers taught them how to build the bridges. The observant Ye Liu Kutsai marveled at the road they made over the frozen heights. "Even in the middle of summer," he wrote in his diary of the march, "masses of ice and snow gather in these mountains. The army had to cut its way through the ice."

They were passing near the bare rock summits of the Roof of the World.

At last Genghis Khan was over the great mountain barrier of mid-Asia. His horsemen survived, although the last of their herds had been killed for meat.

They came down into the bare red plains around Lake Balkash. As the snow melted, hunters went out to search for game. They had come nearly twelve hundred miles from Karakorum.

When they reached growing grass, they left the heavy wagons behind. They formed themselves into four columns and rode swiftly down through the foothills toward the waiting enemy.

Juchi led a flying column off to one side. With a Mongol general as companion to advise him, he and his men sped through a beautiful sunny country. They saw fruit groves, slender towers of minarets rising from clusters of poplars, and cattle grazing on the hillsides. After the winter in the mountains, it all seemed wonderful to the hardy Mongols.

As it happened, the main army of the Moslems, with Muhammad Shah himself, met Juchi's small force. These Moslems, both nobles and common warriors, were brave and good fighters. But it was their first encounter with the dark, leather-clad riders of the Gobi who knew all the tricks of warfare.

All through the day there was a terrible fight, and the monarch of Samarkand never realized that he was facing only a small division of Mongols. Juchi pretended that he had a whole army with him. After dark he lighted many fires as if making camp, and then he led his horsemen away safely.

The next day when Muhammad Shah rode out to the battlefield, he found only the bodies of the dead. He said that he had never before seen men so daring in battle, or so skilled with both bow and sword.

He was really no match for the merciless

Genghis Khan rode up the steps of the great mosque.

He warned the survivors to supply food for his army.

Mongols, let alone Genghis Khan. Their flying columns swam his wide rivers, and their engineers battered breaches in the walls of his fortresses.

It seems that along with their new Chinese siege engines, the Mongols also had the gunpowder they found in Cathay—the Fire that Flies. At that time the Chinese did not know how such explosive powder could be used in cannons. But they had some sort of fireworks and probably rockets. At least the Mongols used the powder in firepots and smoke bombs.

When the Moslems tried to gather together to meet one part of the Mongol horde, they found another column of the strange horsemen circling behind them.

So the baffled Muhammad Shah decided to go back to his strongest cities, Bokhara and Samarkand. He thought that with his great army he could surely defend his twin cities.

He did not know that Genghis Khan had foreseen his decision. For a while the Mongol Khan had disappeared entirely with the center of his horde. Then the Shah heard terrible news.

Genghis Khan was riding toward him swiftly from behind. This Mongol center had disappeared for days in the wastes of the Red Sands Desert, and had gone completely around the Turkish army of the Shah.

This seemed incredible to the harassed Shah. All his planning was to no avail.

The arrogant and proud Shah felt himself trapped, as indeed he was. He did the only thing he could think of: he left his first army to defend the cities while he fled away south with his treasure and courtiers to escape Genghis Khan and to raise another army.

But the Mongols allowed him no time to gather another force. Driving multitudes of captives before them, they stormed or tricked the great cities of Islam into surrender. Then they drove the surviving people out of the walls and sorted them out as carefully as if taking a census.

Able-bodied men they kept to help in building siege works for other cities. Skilled artisans were sent back toward the Mongol country. All who resisted were killed.

The Moslem city people could not understand the doom that had descended on them. A story is told that Genghis Khan, in black lacquered armor and leather-curtained helmet, rode his horse up the steps of the great mosque of Bokhara. He warned the survivors to supply food for his horsemen and grain for his horses.

"Who is this man?" demanded a newcomer, who had not witnessed the capture of the city.

"Hush," whispered those nearest him. "It is the wrath of God that descends on us."

Genghis Khan took pains to make them believe that he was as powerful as fate itself. It was the old Mongol trick of keeping enemies paralyzed with fear. He told the listeners, through scholars who interpreted his words, that their lord the Shah was destined by Heaven to be destroyed because of his sins and pride, and that he, Genghis Khan, was truly the instrument of the wrath of Heaven.

At the same time, he took measures of his own to destroy the fleeing Shah. He sent both Chepé Noyon and Subotai, each with a division of horsemen, to pursue the Moslem monarch like a hunted animal.

14

The Hunting of the Shah

"FOLLOW MUHAMMAD SHAH WHEREVER HE GOES in the world. Find him, alive or dead. I do not think you will find this as hard a task as it seems to you."

That was the order Genghis Khan gave to his two most daring commanders, who by that time were *urkhans,* or marshals. It was a grim task to follow and capture an emperor.

In April of that year, 1220, the two *urkhans* took up the trail with their horsemen. South from Samarkand they headed. By floating on rafts and by swimming they crossed the broad, flooded Amu River.

Muhammad had gone with his family and treasure caskets to the city of Balkh, to wait for his new army. Then he heard that Mongol columns were riding fast on his trail.

He thought first of taking refuge in the mountains of the Afghans behind him. But then he decided he had better journey far away from the terrible horsemen.

So he started west with his caravan, across the waste lands. When he reached the walled city of Nisapur he thought he had put five hundred miles between himself and the pursuing riders.

But he was mistaken. Chepé Noyon, Subotai and their men kept after him. Separating and spreading out, they crossed the desert region, finding grass at the few wells and streams. Every rider had a spare horse. By changing mounts they were able to cover as much as eighty miles a day.

Here in the wastes they lost Muhammad's trail for a while. Then their scouts found out that he was ahead of them. They all turned toward Nisapur.

The anxious Shah learned that he was being followed again. Leaving his family behind, he rode out of the city. He pretended he was going hunting, but he really planned to flee again with a small escort and his gold and jewels.

Against the gates of Nisapur the Mongols stormed. When they discovered that the Shah had left, they turned away from the city to go after him. Now they could ride swiftly west, along the main caravan road.

An army of Persians stood in their way. They smashed through it, but lost the track of the fugitive. Again the two *urkhans* separated as they searched for him. Subotai headed through the gorges up toward the inland Caspian Sea. Chepé Noyon flung out his net of horsemen between the caravan road and the Great Salt Desert of Persia.

They went at such a fast pace that they outrode the very news of their coming.

Muhammad Shah began to be frightened, because he did not know how close the Mongol horsemen might be. He decided to journey to other countries far in the west.

Concealing his treasure in a strong tower, he started along the caravan road with his escort of nobles and warriors. He headed toward Baghdad, where ruled the very Caliph with whom he had quarreled in other days.

He thought no army could follow as fast as his small company could ride. But within a few days he sighted the strange horsemen speeding through the dust at his heels. They scattered his followers and loosed a few arrows at him, not knowing who he was.

On his swift horse Muhammad escaped. Now he was really frightened. Leaving the highway, he doubled back toward the Caspian Sea. Only a few warriors remained with him.

The once powerful Shah had become a fugitive, trying to save his life. And the few men who stayed with him lost respect for him. He was always running away!

One night he found that arrows had passed through his tent. After that he slept out in a small shelter.

"Is there no place on earth," he begged one of his officers, "where I can be safe from the Mongol thunderbolt?"

Friends told him to hurry to the Caspian and take ship to a small island where he could hide. Then after a while his new army could be gathered together to defend him.

So Muhammad disguised himself as a merchant. With only a few servants, he followed a hill trail to a small fishing and trading village on the western shore of the Caspian Sea.

Although tired out and ill, he might still have escaped unknown. But he made a last mistake.

At prayer time in the little mosque by the water's edge, he insisted proudly on reading the prayers, as the Shah.

One man who heard him had suffered at the Shah's hand long before. This Moslem went out and informed the Mongols where he was.

The horsemen scattered another army of Per-

The Moslem went out and told where the Shah was.

sians in their headlong ride to the seaside village. When they arrived, Muhammad was just preparing to embark in a fishing skiff.

Their arrows followed the boat as it drew out from the shore. Some of the men galloped their horses into the water to pursue it.

The boat got away.

Yet the Mongols may be said to have slain Muhammed Shah. Weakened by sickness, this lord of an empire died on his island. So little remained to him that a servant had to give up a shirt to make a shroud for him.

The careful Subotai went back to gather up the Shah's family and treasure to send to Genghis Khan. The two *urkhans* asked for permission to ride on into the unknown west, and a courier brought them the Great Khan's consent.

So they kept on with their amazing march. Exploring the fertile valleys of the vast Caucasus Mountains, they broke down the resistance of the valiant Christian and Moslem mountain people. And they scattered the savage steppe people beyond.

As he rode, Subotai recruited new regiments. His careful Chinese secretaries took a census of all the peoples who submitted. They noted down the locations of silver mines and the routes of caravans.

Behind them, the Mongol courier post carried tidings back and forth. For Genghis Khan planned that after the exploring *urkhans* had passed, his Mongols would come and claim these fertile lands sprinkled with noble cities.

Wandering up into the Russian steppes, the two invincible commanders drove the Kipchaks —desert dwellers—before them. They pushed on toward the setting sun, to the river Dnieper.

There the Russian princes assembled to resist them. From Kiev of the golden domes the princes came with a host of sturdy swordsmen.

But they had no Subotai to lead them.

The wary Mongols tricked the Russians for days by pretending to retreat. Then when the heedless northerners were crossing a small river, the Mongol horsemen turned suddenly and attacked them.

Few of the princes of Kiev or their bold swordsmen survived.

Masters of the steppes, Chepé Noyon and Subotai went down to investigate the shores of the Black Sea. There the daring Chepé Noyon died of illness, and Subotai took over his command.

He was riding on into Europe when an order from Genghis Khan called him back to a council.

By that time Subotai had fought his way across a quarter of the earth. Human strength had been unable to withstand him.

"Have you never heard," a Persian writer of chronicles demanded, "that a band of men from the place where the sun rises overrode the earth to the Caspian Gates? They carried destruction among peoples and sowed death along their way. Then they returned safe and loaded with booty to their master. And this in less than two years!"

15

Reign of Terror

Genghis khan had conquered a new empire in the saddle. But, as Ye Liu Kutsai had warned him, he did not find it easy to hold his conquest.

He had swept over the lands of Islam almost without a stop. Many riders had been lost from the horde. Some of his allies, the wise Uighurs and the Christians of the peaceful Five Cities, were weary and homesick. So he let them return home toward the Gobi.

Part of the horde was off in the west with Sub-otai. Part of it had stayed with Muhuli to rule northern China. The horsemen who remained with the Khan were outnumbered ten to one by the Turkish and Persian warriors, who hated the sight of a Mongol.

And beyond these enemies, to the west, he

discovered that many other warlike and independent people existed. Ye Liu Kutsai had told him that. The wise Cathayan was making a map of this new world. At the same time, he collected the things he prized most—medicines, fruit, and strange writings that told him secrets he wanted to know. He was collecting knowledge while the Mongol Khan took captives and treasure and destroyed cities.

Once Genghis Khan dreamed that he met a strange green animal, with the horns of a deer. This beast seemed to be friendly and tried to talk to him, but the Mongol could not understand his words. So he asked Ye Liu Kutsai to tell him the meaning of the dream.

"The name of this animal is Kotwan," answered the Cathayan, "and he loves living men. He will not come near you if blood has been shed on the ground."

At that time Genghis Khan felt troubled because many of his Mongols, unaccustomed to the summer heat of these southern lands, had fallen sick. But he would not rest content with his victories and march back to the Gobi as Ye Liu Kutsai hoped. Instead, he led his own division up to the hills in the north to hunt and rest where the air was cooler.

He was also anxious because for the first time two of his sons had quarreled bitterly. Juchi, the Guest, and Chagatai, the next oldest, had besieged a great city of Muhammad Shah's. This was a caravan city called Urgench, where the wide river Amu flows into the small sea of Aral.

Juchi wanted to preserve Urgench because it was in the western land that would belong to him. But the harsh Chagatai, who held the post of Master of Punishment, insisted it must be destroyed and its people driven forth because they had resisted the Mongols.

Now Genghis Khan reproved them both for quarreling during a battle, but he ordered that Chagatai should have his way.

"I forbid you all," he told his sons and *urkhans*, "to show mercy to these enemies without an express order from me. Only severity keeps such men obedient. An enemy conquered is not subdued, and will always hate his new master."

Juchi did not like the order of the Khan, and asked permission to return to his steppes in the north.

Genghis Khan meant to rule the stubborn Moslems by terror. Here he showed more savage cruelty than in Cathay.

When the Mongols stormed and sacked Urgench,* they did something to make an end of it forever. They dammed up the Amu above the city, so that the course of the river was changed. It then flowed over the ruins and drowned all the survivors who hid in the cellars. The very name of Urgench vanished after that.

It was then that Genghis Khan summoned Subotai back from the far west. He began a reign of terror. His commanders were told to try to avoid pitched battles. Instead they were to trick enemies into submission and then massacre them.

His youngest son, Tului, had been given the highest post of all, that of Master of War. Being the youngest, Tului—who had spent his life on the road campaigning—got on well enough with his three stern brothers. Wisely, his father had refrained from making either Juchi or Chagatai Master of War, in charge of all the armies.

Tului had disobeyed his father once. He never did it again.

Now Tului was sent back to end the resistance

rising against the Mongols in Persia. He found that it was led by a son of the dead Muhammad Shah. This daring fighter, Jellal ad Din, had sworn never, as long as he lived, to sheath his sword against the Mongols.

In their search for this Prince, Tului's Mongols came to the ancient city of Merv. Far off in the deserts by the River of the Birds, Merv was famous for its libraries and beautiful gardens. After their first storm failed to capture this city, the crafty Mongols tricked it to its doom.

They waited in their encampment to see if the defenders would send out a spokesman. Only one unarmed man came out—an *imam,* or religious master.

This *imam* explained that he was not an official of the city but had been sent out by the Governor, whose name was Merik. The Mongols treated him courteously and sent him back safely.

Reassured by their treatment of the *imam,* Merik himself appeared from the gate, with servants bearing rich gifts of silver and embroidered robes.

Tului took the gifts, politely sent back a fine

robe of honor, and invited Merik to his own tent to dine. The Governor wanted to talk about terms for the city, and the cunning Tului convinced him that his own life would surely be spared.

"Summon forth your friends and great lords," Tului suggested, after feasting the relieved Governor. "There is work for them to do here and I will honor them as well as you."

Merik accordingly dispatched a servant to bring out his chosen companions, who joined him at the feast carpet. Next, Tului asked for a list of the six hundred richest men of Merv, and the Governor and his intimates obediently wrote out the names of the wealthiest landholders and merchants. They thought this was the Mongol way of coming to terms and did not suspect the trick.

Before the eyes of the horrified Merik, all his noble companions were strangled by Mongol warriors. After that, the list of the six hundred wealthy men was taken to the gate of Merv by a Mongol officer, who said the Governor wanted all the six hundred to come out. Because Merik and his friends had written down the names themselves, the wealthy men believed the officer and came out.

As these men emerged, Mongol swordsmen appeared as if to guard them, and took possession of the gate. Now the anxious people inside no longer had leaders to advise them. And Tului, outside, had all the wealthy men of Merv in his hands.

Mongol horsemen rode into the open gate, still pretending to carry out orders of the Governor. They forced all the inhabitants to collect their valuable belongings and march out of the city. This went on for four days, while Tului himself sat and watched on a raised throne covered with cloth-of-gold.

His officers singled out all Persian officers and ordered them to go before the Mongol prince. They were made to kneel and their heads were cut off.

No one was left to lead any resistance against the Mongols.

While Tului watched, the Mongols forced the multitude of captives to lie down and then carried off their belongings. After that, the Mongols killed everyone except four hundred crafts-

One by one the Persian princes were executed.

men needed by the horde, and some children.

The six hundred wealthy men fared little better. They were tortured until they revealed where they had hidden their most prized possessions.

Then the Mongols searched through the empty houses and pulled down the walls. The only people alive in Merv were those who had hidden underground. After a few days some riders of the horde came back to find and kill these also.

So, without any injury to themselves, the

Mongols emptied Merv by their cunning tricks.

At another place where the people had hidden away, the Mongols tricked the inhabitants by pretending to ride on. But they forced a muezzin to give the Moslem call to prayer from a mosque. Hearing this, the people came out of hiding—to be caught and killed.

From the Roof of the World to far-off Baghdad the survivors lived in such fear that most of them no longer tried to protect themselves. The very sight of a nomad horseman made them helpless.

"I was on the road with seventeen other men," one of them related. "We saw a Tartar horseman coming up to us. He ordered us to tie up our companions—each man to bind another's arms behind his back. The others were beginning to obey him when I said to them, 'This man is alone. Let's kill him and escape.'

"They replied, 'We are too much afraid.'

" 'But this man will kill you,' I said.

"Still no one dared disobey the Tartar. So I killed him with a blow of my knife. Then we all ran away and saved ourselves."

Genghis Khan was holding all the Moslem lands in fear. Yet he had not been able to hunt down the daring Prince, Jellal ad Din. Gathering an army of determined horsemen, Jellal ad Din defeated for the first time a Mongol division commanded by a general named Shikaku.

This was a blow to the Great Khan, but he did not show any anger against Shikaku. Many years before, Genghis Khan had been snowed in with a few companions. They had no food, but this same Shikaku had gone out alone into the blizzard and brought back two deer. The Mongol Khan remembered this. "Shikaku was careless," he said, "because he had become accustomed to success. Now he will take care to be wary as a wolf at all times."

And he took the defeated general back over the ground of the battle to point out how he had fallen into Jellal ad Din's trap.

Secretly the old Khan admired the brave Turkish Prince for his courage. And he started to hunt down this champion himself.

16

The Speaker-to-Heaven

EXCEPT FOR JELLAL AD DIN'S ARMY, GENGHIS Khan prevailed over his Moslem enemies. This was chiefly because he held fast to all the highways. The surviving Moslems no longer had many cities. Since they were obliged to keep away from the roads, they had to hide out in mountains or distant villages. Thus, they could not easily reach their friends who were in other places.

On the other hand the Mongols, using the roads, kept in touch with each other and all that was happening.

Genghis Khan had an effective system of communication. Wherever he led the horde, he set up the swift horse-post behind him. It was like a telegraph wire and railroad track stretching all the way back to the Gobi and Cathay.

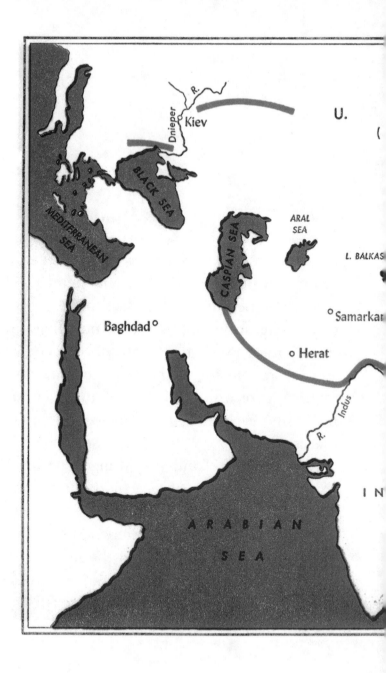

U.

(

Dnieper R.

Kiev

BLACK SEA

MEDITERRANEAN SEA

CASPIAN SEA

ARAL SEA

L. BALKAS

°Samarkar

Baghdad°

°Herat

Indus R.

IN

ARABIAN

SEA

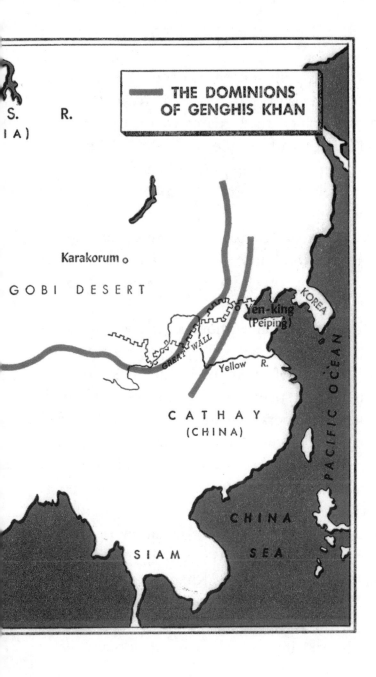

THE DOMINIONS
OF GENGHIS KHAN

S. R.
IA)

Karakorum o

GOBI DESERT

KOREA

GREAT WALL

o Yen-king
(Peiping)

Yellow R.

CATHAY
(CHINA)

PACIFIC OCEAN

CHINA

SIAM   SEA

Mongol post stations linked the roads together. Herds of spare horses were kept at each station. Armed road guards camped by the station houses, to keep the roads clear of enemies.

Past these stations plodded endless caravans, taking silver and precious things back to the Mongol homes. Past them, in the opposite direction, journeyed bands of young warriors eager to join the horde. They were envious of the veterans returning home with trophies of swords, jewels and armor.

Up to these station houses galloped the couriers of the Khan, the bells on their girdles giving warning of their approach. Tied to their girdles these speeding riders carried gold tubes in which papers bearing written orders had been curled and sealed. Couriers from the Khan himself could stop any other traveler, even a high commander or *tarkhan,* to take his horse to ride on. They covered a hundred and fifty miles a day without rest. And other riders had to wheel out of their way as they sped past crying out, "For the Great Khan!"

"The speed at which they go is marvelous," Marco Polo related in the time of the Khan's grandsons. "By them the emperor obtains news from places ten days' journey off in one day and night. The clerk at each post writes down the time of each courier's arrival and departure. A horse is always waiting for them, ready saddled and fresh, so they can mount and go at full speed. Even when the messengers go through roadless stretches, they find camps and horses waiting for them.

"At the stations which they call the Horse-Post-Houses, there is a large and handsome building for the riders to rest in. Here the rooms are furnished with fine beds covered with silk."

Past these posts journeyed other strange figures: yellow-hatted lamas, swinging prayer wheels; slant-eyed Buddhist pilgrims striding down from the heights of Tibet; and black-robed Nestorian Christian priests murmuring their prayers.

For Genghis Khan was tolerant of these servants of an invisible power, that of the Sky, or Heaven. Even while struggling with the Moslems, he gave their *imams* authority to judge people and to spare those condemned to death.

Often he summoned these venerable men to talk with him. In his mind there were only two invincible powers, that of the Khan upon earth and that of the Sky.

As he grew older he began to wonder more and more what went on beyond the Gate of the Sky. Once he said to Ye Liu Kutsai, "I have acted without knowledge of what to do rightly. But what do I care for the lives of strange men?"

Then a courier who bore a gold tiger-tablet sped up the post roads. This rider dismounted at the door of a thatched house in distant China. At this obscure home lived an elderly revered man named Ch'ang Ch'un. He was a Taoist, one who might know the secrets of Heaven.

To Ch'ang Ch'un the Great Khan had sent a message. "From the waste lands of the north I have come forth. I eat common food and wear only one coat. The people who dwell in felt tents are my children. I share their struggles in battle. In seven years I have conquered the forces of the earth for them.

"Yet I fear that I am not able to rule wisely. To cross a river we make use of rafts and poles. So to govern an empire we must make use of wise men. You are, like the clouds, above such men. Do not be afraid, but think of the welfare of many people and come to my side, across the mountains and sandy deserts. Tell me how my life can be prolonged."

Across the length of the continent, Ch'ang Ch'un, the Taoist, was brought by couriers to Genghis Khan. When he stood before the old Mongol he showed no fear.

"You who obey no king's command," said Genghis Khan, "have come to me. I am glad."

It seemed to the Khan that this silent priest might be a true Speaker-to-Heaven, and might have the secret that would preserve his own life for years.

"It is not by my will," said Ch'ang Ch'un boldly, "but by the will of Heaven that I have come."

That pleased the Mongol.

Then the Taoist explained that he brought no charm to preserve life. "Live at peace," he advised Genghis Khan. "Cease from destroying the lives of others."

Soon after that the Khan was hunting a boar when he was thrown from his horse and injured. The wild boar, however, did not charge him on the ground but swerved aside.

"That was a sign of warning," the Taoist told

him. "You have done ill to take life. If Heaven had not prevented, the boar would have gored you."

The old Mongol thought this over and answered, "I understood that myself. I know your advice is good. But we Mongols have grown accustomed from our earliest years to hunt. It is not easy to change our habits."

Two months later he was in the saddle again, hunting. Indeed it was not easy to change his ways. Yet he worried because he had been wounded often, and might not have many years to live. After he was gone, who would hold his four strong sons together? One night during the hunt, he called Chagatai, Ogodai and Tului to his seat by the fire.

Juchi had asked permission to stay away from the hunt, in the west. This grieved Genghis Khan. He had cherished Juchi ever since the days of poverty when Bortay had nothing but dough with which to line a cradle for the child.

"Remember well the words of Ch'ang Ch'un," he told the other three. "To strive against one of your own blood is to put out the fire on the hearth."

Then he told them what he meant to do. "I

shall give each of you a nation to rule. But one must rule over the other three, and they must obey him as you obey me now."

Which of the four did he mean to leave over the others? Chagatai? They could not tell. Chagatai and the two others became angry when they heard that Juchi too would have a kingdom.

Perhaps Genghis Khan had been thinking of his sons more than of himself when he sent for the Speaker-to-Heaven, Ch'ang Ch'un.

Perhaps he had wanted to learn how to preserve peace for the four sons of Bortay in the years to come. For himself he knew there could be no peace.

17

The Last Battle

FAR TO THE SOUTHEAST REBELLION WAS BREAK-ing out. As Genghis Khan had expected, new armies gathered around the defiant Jellal ad Din.

The Moslem world was rising against its conqueror. Cities drove out their Mongol garrisons. Along the highroads appeared the green banners of the Moslems. Horsemen rode down from the mountain villages to rally to the banners.

Worst of all for the Mongols, they gathered by tens of thousands in the east, where the high mountain ranges of the Afghans protected them. The Afghans joined with the Turks of Jellal ad Din, as did fugitive Persians and volunteers from India. They outnumbered the weary Mongols.

How Genghis Khan must have wished that Subotai were at his side! But the invincible *urkhan* was still on the way back from Russia.

The old Mongol knew that Tului alone could not deal with such danger. He sent Tului south to besiege the nearest city of the eastern mountains, walled Herat. With the rest of the horde —no more than some thirty thousand—he took the field himself, heading straight toward the rising sun to find his antagonist, Jellal ad Din.

Up into the bare heights of the mountains he galloped with his veterans. His scouts told him that Jellal ad Din had been seen at lofty Bamyan, near the Father of Mountains.

When the Mongols climbed the trails that led through the clouds to Bamyan, they came upon a strange sight. Giant stone figures sat beneath the cliff of Bamyan, as if watching ceaselessly over the lands and people below them.

These were ancient statues of Buddha. The far-traveling Mongols had found others like them in the temples of Cathay and in the Gobi Desert. It seemed as if the ancient gods were watching them wherever they went.

Never had the Mongols been put to a greater test. The defenders of Bamyan had cleared away all the loose boulders that might have been used by engines to batter down their walls. Their own machines threw out burning naphtha on the Mongols who climbed to the assault. After a grandson cherished by Genghis Khan was killed, the Khan himself joined the storming of the walls that went on without ceasing to the crashing of kettledrums.

Meanwhile, the scouting army of Shikaku was routed, as has been explained, by the daring Jellal ad Din, who had been careful to keep his army outside Bamyan.

When at last this citadel of the mountains was taken and torn down, Genghis Khan left it without a day's delay to ride after the Moslem host. As he rode, he rallied the survivors of Shikaku's division. Instead of blaming them for their failure, he praised them for their bravery.

Like hounds on a scent, the Mongols raced through the rock ravines of the heights.

Cautiously the Moslems drew back to another citadel, Ghazni. They were the stronger army but they did not have a Genghis Khan to lead them. The old Khan gained on them.

The Afghans became afraid and left Jellal ad

Din. He decided to retreat to India, to gather new allies.

He hurried through the passes of the last mountains and came down into the great valley of the river Indus. But the Mongols were hard after him. At Ghazni they had been five days behind him. As he galloped to the Indus they were only half a day behind. They came on without stopping even to cook food for a meal.

When at last he reached the steep bank of the river, Jellal ad Din searched anxiously for a way across the flooded Indus. He had come to a place where the bank was steep and the water deep. There was no time to go elsewhere to search for a ford.

Hunted out of his own lands, the Moslem Prince turned at bay to face his pursuers. His host held the level ground between a bend in the river and a high ridged mountain on his left. Jellal ad Din ordered the boats along the bank behind him to be destroyed, so that none of his men would think of fleeing.

He had to defeat Genghis Khan or be destroyed himself.

At daybreak he sighted the horned standards

of the pagan nomads moving toward him. Fiercely he threw his fine horsemen forward in attack.

It seemed at first as if he were victorious. Time after time the Moslem charges broke through the masses of leather-clad Mongols.

Finally Genghis Khan had only one fresh body of warriors to throw into the battle. Instead of leading these forward himself, he gave them to a *noyon* with orders to circle away and climb the ridged mountain off at the side. This was like the time that Guïldar took the standard to the hill in the Gobi long before.

The *noyon* led a climb up cliff tracks so steep that some of his men slipped and fell to their deaths. But he made his way over the mountain ridge and charged down behind the Moslems.

No sooner had he done so than Genghis Khan led an attack from the other side. The tired Moslems, who thought they had been pursuing the enemy, found themselves almost surrounded and cut off from the river.

Desperately Jellal ad Din rallied his disordered army and led a charge against the oncoming Mongols. Flights of short, swift arrows from deadly bows drove back the courageous Moslem

On the cliff some slipped and fell to their death.

swordsmen. But their bravery was to no avail against the sagacity of the Mongols.

They were herded about like animals unable to break through the hunters' ring. Then, hopelessly, Jellal ad Din tried to lead the survivors back to the river. When he reached the steep bank, there were no more than seven hundred left to follow him. All the boats were gone.

Realizing that his army was lost, the Prince threw off his heavy chain mail. He tore one of the green banners from its pole, picked up his sword, and jumped to the saddle of a fresh horse.

After he forced his charger to the edge of the bank, he made the horse jump down into the current. Breasting the swift current, horse and rider swam to the distant shore.

Genghis Khan had given orders that the Prince be taken alive. As the Mongols gained the bank, the Khan saw Jellal ad Din climb out on the far shore, sword in hand. For a moment he gazed in silence. Then he exclaimed, instinctively, in praise:

"Fortunate is the father of such a son!"

Some of his Mongols wanted to swim their horses after the lone Moslem rider, but the Khan would not allow that. The next day he went on to a ford, and sent a whole division across the river to pursue the Prince through India. He gave the command of this pursuit to the *noyon* who had won the battle by riding over the roadless mountain.

This *noyon* galloped headlong down into India, ravaging Multan and Lahore. For a while he kept on the trail of the fugitive, then lost him among the multitudes on the road to Delhi.

The great heat of the Indian plain astonished the riders from the Gobi. It made them turn back, and they reported to the Khan, "The heat of this place slays men, and the water does not quench thirst."

Jellal ad Din survived. But he was now a man without a country. No other great army rallied to him, and he could fight the Mongols only as a partisan, leading small bands.

Genghis Khan had won his final victory at the Indus River. He had overcome all human resistance from the shores of the Pacific to the Russian steppes, from Herat in the southern desert to the ice-bound tundras beneath the Gate of the Sky.

Now he could give the order for all his divisions to gather together to march home.

It seemed to him that the shortest way back was to go straight from India. But here he found a barrier that could not be crossed—the snow summits of the Himalayas.

So, carrying along the spoils of northern India, he made a great detour, retracing his way to Samarkand. From there the familiar caravan and post roads led back to the Gobi.

The last thing Genghis Khan did before leaving the sun-warmed lands of Islam was to appoint Moslem governors to care for them in his absence. He knew that he would never come back to these lands. His sons, however, would return to rule them.

Out over the post roads he sent a summons to all Mongol commanders to come to a great council on the river Syr.

18

Council of the Conquerors

THERE WERE PRAIRIES BY THE WIDE RIVER SYR.
Not a house was to be seen.

Instead, water fowl filled the marshes by the
river bank, pheasants flitted through the high
grass, and antelope raced away to the edge of
the sky. This was the place chosen by Genghis
Khan for the meeting of all his Mongols after so
many years of war.

When spring warmed these meadows, they
rode in from all the points of the compass. *Urkhans* arrived with armored warriors tossing
their lances into the air; silvered chain mail
jangled on the horses as well as on the men.
Tarkhans approached, followed by streams of
white camels plodding under loads of precious
things.

Down from the snow heights came Chagatai, who had bridged the roads to Cathay. Wide-horned yaks drew his carts after him.

With ox-drawn *kibitkas* trailing him, the good-natured Ogodai rode in from the homeland by the Mountain of Power.

After him appeared silk-clad Uighur chieftains of the Th'ian Shan, and the Lion King of the Christian folk. At the same time came lamas from Tibet, envoys of the Caliph of Baghdad, proud ambassadors of the hard-riding Turkomans, and the sultans of Delhi. Silver and jewels gleamed in the harnesses of their horses.

The Mongols were coming in from the ends of the earth.

No longer did they clothe themselves in the leather and sheepskin of the Gobi. Satin robes and cloth-of-gold covered them.

All of them brought gifts to the pavilion of Genghis Khan, where the yak-tail standard stood. The Khan received herds of swift horses, mountains of furs, wagon trains of gold and silver work, vessels of glass, and thrones of turquoise and rubies—undreamed-of wealth from conquered courts.

"Never," wrote one of the Persian scribes,

"was such splendor seen in one place before."

Inside the Khan's pavilion splendid things appeared. Honey mead and the wines of Shiraz, instead of the mare's milk of the nomads, stayed the thirst of the guests. Peacock plumes swayed above screens of ivory and gold while captive girls of Cathay sang softly.

On the raised seat behind the fires, however, a gray cloth of animal hair had been stretched. It was there to remind the visitors that he who sat above them was still a nomad, still a dweller of the waste lands.

"I have gained this mastery," the old Khan reminded them, "by carrying out our Law. Live ye henceforth by the Law."

He had planned to have his people take for themselves the wealth of the outer courts and cities. But he did not want them to change their old ways or to leave their deserts.

He wanted his family, the Golden Family, to direct the army and the ministers, who in turn would rule the nomad folk of the tents, who in their turn would be masters of all the subjected peoples.

But the wayward Juchi did not come to the council. Instead he sent from his steppes a herd of thousands of swift horses and a message that he was too sick to ride.

"Is it true," Genghis Khan asked the messenger, "that my son Juchi is sick?"

"When I left his side," the Mongol officer answered carefully, "he was hunting."

His three other sons heard of this and came before the Khan. "Do you still hold him to be like us?" they demanded. "Now he rebels against you."

Juchi had disobeyed the Khan's summons to council. And the punishment for that was death.

Troubled at heart, the old Khan pondered. At length he announced that at the end of the council the Mongol horde would march to the north, to make war upon Juchi and his followers if they had rebelled.

Then he sent a courier of his own speeding to the west. This courier carried an order to Subotai, hundreds of miles away. The order was to find Juchi and bring him to the council. Subotai had never failed to carry out an order.

Days passed while they waited for news from the west. Then riders were sighted coming in along the river. The standards of an army showed behind them.

It was Subotai, bringing captive Russians and Kipchaks. At last the victorious *urkhan* rode to the tent of the master he had not seen for three years. He brought word that Juchi had died of sickness in the steppes, and he brought with him a silent youth, Batu, the son of the dead man.

Genghis Khan said, "In spite of all we can do, death will come." He gave Juchi's lands to Batu, but he grieved because Juchi had not lived to come to the last council.

He welcomed, too, a nine-year-old boy, Kubilai, the son of Tului, Master of War. With Kubilai the old Mongol liked to talk. And he found that the boy knew more about books and the ways of court life than about hunting. Ye Liu Kutsai had seen to that.

"The words of Kubilai," Genghis said approvingly, "are full of wisdom."

He did not foresee the change that might come from such education. His grandsons would grow up to think differently about war and human life and their own possessions.

But Ye Liu Kutsai understood very well that this would happen. He dared advise the old Khan about something else. "Your children and *tarkhans,*" he suggested, "will have in their hands all the reins of warfare and the keeping of the post roads through your dominion. Yet to act as judges they should have men of wisdom, and to gather taxes they should have the mandarins of Cathay who understand such things."

It seemed reasonable to Genghis Khan that each one should carry out the work he knew best. And he agreed. The old Khan wanted the sage of Cathay to keep on helping his sons.

For he meant Tului, the youngest, to be chief among them, while the mild Ogodai ruled the homelands, and Chagatai became master of mid-Asia, where the council was held.

The oldest grandson, Batu Khan, would be supreme in the west, in the steppes of Russia.

More than in anyone else, however, he put his trust in Subotai. It soothed the weary old Khan to have his companion at his side again. When the others had gone from his pavilion and only the young warriors waited silently at the entrance, Genghis Khan bade Subotai to remain seated by the fire.

"Tell me of the strange lands in the west ruled by the Christian kings and the great Pope," he requested of Subotai.

The old Khan listened as Subotai told of the West.

In the minds of both of them it became clear that this place called Europe must also be invaded and subdued, so that there would remain no antagonists to the Golden Family.

"Guide my sons to do that," Genghis Khan told Subotai. "Keep, unfailing, at the side of the boy Batu."

Subotai wished the great *ordu,* or horde, to

turn to the far west immediately, to carry out his task. However, Genghis Khan would not agree to do that. After being away for so many years, he longed to see his own rivers and the Mountain of Power again.

One night the old Mongol heard the guards whispering at his tent entrance. He rose and went out to learn what had stirred them.

The night was cold, and a north wind swayed the banners of the encampment. His young warriors pointed into the wind.

Far off along the northern skyline lights rose and fell. They seemed to leap up against the stars.

Genghis Khan knew that spirits were dancing there, in the Gate of the Sky. Not for years had his eyes beheld them.

At once he gave orders for his *ordu* to begin the march toward the northern lights, toward his home.

19

End of the Road

GENGHIS KHAN WAS NOT DESTINED TO SPEND HIS
last years at rest in his homeland. He led the
great *ordu* back to Karakorum, where Bortay
and the Mongol women waited. For only one
season did he ride around his familiar grazing
grounds.

Then he was off to battle again. Muhuli, his
commander in Cathay, had died, and southern
China, under the Sung emperors, still remained
unconquered.

Moreover, beyond the sand deserts down by
Tibet, the troublesome lords of Hsia had gathered together the remnants of peoples to resist
the Mongols. Also, the cities of the Golden Emperor were trying to throw off the Mongol yoke.

So the dreaded Khan found more antagonists waiting in the east. His task of conquest was not ended.

He sent Subotai to take command in Cathay and to subdue the cities.

Against this Ye Liu Kutsai dared to protest. "If such people as these be slain, how then will they work for you or make wealth for your sons?"

The old Khan pondered. "You will be master of all subject peoples. And you will serve my sons faithfully."

In this way, he was willing to give authority to the sage Cathayan. Yet he would not refrain from the final conquest of Cathay. Subotai went on his way with part of the armies.

Genghis Khan himself headed over the deserts toward the Hsia rebels. At his coming the King of Hsia drew back into his ice-covered hills and sent word to the Mongols, protesting that he was their friend and asking them to forget what had happened in the past.

"Say to your master," Genghis Khan replied to the envoys, "that I have no wish to remember what is past. I will find out now if he is my friend."

Riding on through frozen swamps, he found the host of Hsia no sort of friends; they were

Tului found his father lying by the yurt fire.

waiting to attack him. His veteran horsemen withstood the onset. Through the night they pursued the remnants of foemen, speeding across ice-filled rivers.

The King of Hsia escaped through snow-drifted gorges to hide in the mountain summits. Still Genghis Khan followed after him.

Up in the heights the cold was so great that even the fur-clad Mongols could not move against the wind that swept the gorges. And Genghis Khan stayed long in his domed tent, as if grieving. At night the flames of the north leaped high in the sky.

Hour after hour the old Khan sat still as if meditating. Then he sent couriers for Tului. The windstorm ceased, and the horde moved on to the shelter of a forest. Here their master gave the command to halt.

When Tului hastened in over the mountain trail, he found his father lying by the *yurt* fire wrapped in a gray cloth and sable furs.

"It is clear to me now," he said, "that I must leave everything to you."

To Tului and his officers who gathered about him, he told how Subotai must carry on the war against the last defiant cities of Cathay. He told them how they must deal with the fugitive King of Hsia. Then, last of all, he told how his invincible armies were to be divided among his sons and Batu.

He had been sick for some time, and now the sickness drained away his life.

But it was not immediately made known that the Great Khan was dead. The standard stood in its accustomed place. Officers came and went through the tent entrance.

A lance was thrust in the ground before the entrance. And the young guardsmen kept ordinary folk away from the tent. Genghis Khan had commanded this.

A message of friendship was sent to the hiding place of the King of Hsia. It invited him and his officers and court to come to the Mongol camp.

When they appeared, they were given robes of honor and gifts. Then, wearing their new robes, they were led to a pavilion and seated at a feast among Mongol officers.

There every last one of them was slain. Thus, after his death, did Genghis Khan dispose of his enemy.

When the snows melted, the horde started home. From all directions horsemen came in to march beside the cart that carried the body of the Great Khan.

They could hardly believe that the tall old man with the wide, bent shoulders and the gray cat's eyes lay motionless within the casket jolting over the dirt road. "He was like an eagle flying past, seeking its prey," they said to each other. "Never before did he have a home or abiding place."

On this journey across the red soil of China

the Mongols killed all the country people who had seen the death cart passing. Perhaps they did not wish any enemies to know that Genghis Khan had ceased to live. Perhaps they wanted the spirits of the slain to accompany the dreaded Khan in his journey out of the world into the Sky.

They rode back to the prairies and the cold winds of the north. At each Mongol encampment the women, leading the children, came out to mourn.

"In the time of grass our Khan nourished us," they wailed. "In the winter's wind, our Khan warmed us. Now he is gone, and the sweet water has left our rivers, the shade has vanished from the trees of our gardens."

When the cart had passed the encampments of all of his family, it was taken away secretly. The riders who took it covered their trail. They covered the grave they dug in a grove of trees.

Perhaps it was in the grove that he had admired by the Mountain of Power. The Mongol riders would not reveal the place.

For a while some of them remained to stand guard over it, as if it had been his tent in the days of his power. Then they went away.

From time to time, even until now, searchers have claimed that they have found the tomb of Genghis Khan. But it has never been found. As you see, there was nothing like a tomb—only the grave in the earth overgrown with trees.

What remained upon the earth for generations was the fear inspired by his name.

20

The Mongol Masters

No OTHER MAN, EXCEPT ALEXANDER THE GREAT
long before the time of Genghis Khan, ever
made such a change in the world during one life-
time.

His commands were obeyed even after his
death. It was as if he still sat on the raised throne
of the council of the Mongol khans.

Everything written down in his Law was carried out by the generation that followed him.
Subotai and Tului began the conquest of the
teeming cities of the strong Sung empire in
southern China.

Then Subotai the Invincible turned west
again. With Batu Khan, he swept over the Russian princes and over the brave Poles and Hun-
garians. He got as far as Vienna.

The people of France and Germany became fearful that the dreaded Mongols would ride on to them. In their churches they prayed to be spared the fury of the "Tartars," as they called the nomad conquerors. But as it happened, Subotai and Batu Khan turned back from Europe because they were summoned east to a council in the Gobi.

So the Europe of our ancestors was spared the terror of a Mongol conquest. The Russian people, however, were held under the yoke of the nomad khans for nearly three hundred years.

Because they had to live so long under the rule of these "Tartars," the Russians of that day became very different from our own ancestors farther west.

As Genghis Khan had done in the east, Batu Khan—who was called "The Splendid"—gathered wealth from the west and took it away to where his herds and tent cities wandered along the banks of the river Volga. His people became known as the Golden Horde.

All the frontiers of the eastern world which had existed before Genghis Khan had been wiped out. We will never know what Russia would have been, or China would have become.

or the fine Moslem kingdoms would have achieved, if it had not been for the Mongols.

For the younger Mongol leaders returned to the sunny lands beyond Samarkand. Jellal ad Din fought them vainly. They conquered and humbled the Caliph of Baghdad, and came almost within sight of Jerusalem.

There they exchanged messages with some of our ancestors, the crusaders who were holding fast to their castles in the Holy Land. In fact, letters passed back and forth between the strange Mongol khans and the Pope in Rome.

Perhaps this might not have been accomplished if it had not been for the wise advice of Ye Liu Kutsai and the other learned men both of Cathay and Islam. As Subotai really became the leader in war, Ye Liu Kutsai became the leader of activities in peace.

Although the Mongol conquests brought terror to millions of human beings and destroyed so many thriving cities, the Mongol peace that came after gave help in many ways. Churches were not harmed, and priests of all faiths were allowed to do all they desired.

The post roads stretched across most of the Old World. Couriers carried valuable things as well as messages from the unknown east to the frontiers of our ancestors.

There was a saying in Russia then that "A dog can not bark without the permission of Batu Khan." And it was also said that a young girl alone could carry a sack of gold safely from the river Don to Khanbaligh, the City of the Khans, called Cambaluc by our ancestors. That could hardly be done today.

Merchants began to send their caravans over the new roads. It may not be true that in this way the secrets of gunpowder and the printing of books reached our ancestors in Europe, but certainly many useful things did reach them.

For the first time the Europeans really discovered how far the world extended to the east. Many of them set out over the post roads, to journey past Samarkand to fabulous Cathay.

21

Last Court of the Nomads

WE HAVE THE STORY OF ONE OF THE FIRST MEN to risk their lives on the long journey to the great Khan. He was a barefoot friar, stout as Friar Tuck, from a small town in Holland. The sturdy Friar William of Rubruk carried a sealed letter from the King of the French, who happened to be Saint Louis.

A generation after the death of Genghis Khan, Friar William made his way across the steppes of Russia. After riding three days in a clumsy cart, he came to the first road guard of "Tartars," as he called them.

"When I joined them I thought I had stepped into a new world. We never slept under a roof of a house, but always in the open, or under our carts. Nor did we see any town.

"The houses of these Tartars are tents, some of them thirty feet across, with paintings on the inside of the cloth. These tents are carried about on wagons. Once I measured the space between the wheel ruts of a wagon and found it to be twenty feet.

"The court of a rich Mongol is made up of two or three hundred such carts. And one girl is able to drive twenty of them, fastened together one behind the other. For the ground is level and they follow easily as fast as the oxen can walk.

"They all wear silks and cottons from Persia in summer, and fine furs from Russia in winter. Their garments are lined with silk shag, which is light, soft and warm. They have falcons which they carry on their right arms, with a thong fastened about its neck. For they are all expert in hunting, and gain much of their food from the chase."

On the road Friar William was given a strong horse because he was a stout man. Each day he had to ride a great distance with the cavalcade of nomads. Not until nightfall was he allowed to dismount to eat a meal of barley cooked with meat.

There were many others speeding along the

trail over the steppes. The friar met with a Templar from Cyprus, and a Hungarian priest who could speak with the Tartars. In this kingdom of the grasslands he found his guards to be proud people, believing themselves superior to others.

In fact they consented to escort the bold voyager from Holland only because they were taking him to Batu Khan, lord of the Golden Horde, on his way to the great Khan at "Cambaluc."

At last they came in sight of the gray river Volga. At a Russian village they ferried the friar across to the east bank, where the Tartars grazed their herds.

"We drifted down the current of the Volga to his court. There we were amazed at the magnificence of his encampment. The tents appeared to stretch everywhere to a vast distance.

"First we were taken to a Moslem who led us to a great pavilion with doors lying open to the south where a multitude of people waited.

"They called this the Ordu or center of their habitations. And there the Khan must always be, in the center of his people.

"Then we were led into the pavilion, while our guards cautioned us not to touch the tent

Batu was seated on a long broad couch like a bed.

ropes or threshold. We went in barefoot with our heads uncovered. And those within stared at us, as at a strange spectacle.

"Batu was seated on a long broad couch, like a bed. It had a covering of gilt, raised three steps from the ground. One of his ladies had a place beside him, while his chief men sat all around him.

"By the entrance stood a bench set with jeweled cups of gold and silver containing mare's milk. Our guides cautioned us not to speak before Batu spoke.

"For a time he looked at us steadily—a strong, ruddy man. I repeated a prayer to myself, silently.

"Then he signed for me to speak. My guide cautioned me to bend down upon my knee. Yet Batu bade drink be given me, and this is a sign of honor among them. He also desired me to look up at him. Because these people take it to be a sign of ill fortune if anyone holds his head down before them."

In this way the envoy of the French King humbled himself before a grandson of Genghis Khan. The power of the Mongols stretched like an invisible empire from the banks of the Danube to the Yangtze River, where Kubilai had gone to rule.

Then Friar William was taken over the winter roads to the City of the Khan itself, in the Mongol homeland. There another son of Tului ruled as the great Khan. There the stout friar met with Christian folks, as if it had been a crossroads of the world. Indeed, he found Nestorian priests, and a woman from Metz who had a fine home, and a goldsmith from Paris, and a grand prince of Russia.

Chinese and Armenian and Persian teachers helped all those who spoke different languages to talk with one another. The French goldsmith was making out of pure silver a tree from which rice wine and honey mead flowed when a trumpet sounded at the tree's top. He also made a small altar for the bold friar.

Genghis Khan had foretold that his descendants would desire such things, and that after a time they would forget his commands. It happened as he had said.

Far off in Persia, the son of Tului who ruled there did not want to leave the luxury of his court to journey back to the court of the great Khan in the desert. It was the same way with Batu, who stayed with his Golden Horde on the Volga.

Although the armies commanded by the Mongols became greater than before, the family of Genghis Khan no longer held together. All of the grandsons had been taught to think for themselves and to desire the civilization over which each one ruled.

There was no longer a Subotai to unite them in war. So in the end the teaching of the wise Ye Liu Kutsai prevailed over the Law of Genghis Khan.

When Kubilai, youngest of the grandsons, became the great Khan, he abandoned the city in the desert and went to dwell within Cathay. After he had lived in the palaces of Yen-king within the Great Wall, he became more like the Chinese—very different from his kinsmen of the Golden Horde.

After separating in this manner, the Mongol lords of the world began to fight among themselves. Then, too, they turned to different religions. Those in China became Buddhists, and those in Persia became Moslems, while those in the Mongol homeland followed the shamans and lamas as their descendants do to-day.

So in the end the outer civilizations proved to be stronger than the barbaric power of the Mongols.

Yet it was Genghis Khan who broke down the barriers of the Dark Ages and put far Asia in touch with Christian Europe.

Index

179